THE SELF IN PILGRIMAGE

The SELF In PILGRIMAGE

Earl A. Loomis, Jr., M.D.

HARPER & ROW, PUBLISHERS
New York, Evanston and London

THE SELF IN PILGRIMAGE

Copyright © 1960 by Earl A. Loomis, Jr.

Printed in the United States of America

E-P

Library of Congress catalog card number: 60-11781

To
My Father

CONTENTS

FOREWORDS

by REINHOLD NIEBUHR
and KENNETH E. APPEL

Professor Earl A. Loomis, Jr., who is the Director of the Program in Psychiatry and Religion at Union Theological Seminary in New York, has given us in this book a remarkably fruitful analysis of the human self, which validates the cooperation of theological and psychiatric studies. He has drawn on religious and psychodynamic insights to give us a very telling analysis of problems of human selfhood. He draws particularly on the theological traditions of the Hebraic-Christian stream of thought to emphasize both the unity of the self in body, mind, and spirit, and the significance of individual selfhood as contrasted with the mystic desire and ambition to eliminate the ego. In his analysis of self-discovery he has combined both religious and psychiatric insights to plumb the depths of the labyrinthian self with its good and evil possibilities and with its fear of coming to terms with both of these possibilities. In dealing with the image of the self and the image of God in terms of the religious doctrine that the self is made in the image of God and in terms of psychiatric fact that the self usually makes an image of God in terms of itself, he has again given us some very fruitful insights.

He has shown that the Hebraic-Christian interpretation makes

for an emphasis not only upon individual selfhood but upon the
necessity of the self in community and the inevitability of the
self's involvement in history. In his chapters on the development of the self from childhood to maturity he has particularly
validated this necessary co-operation between the psychiatric
and religious insights. He deals honestly with the sexuality of
the child, with the necessity of emancipating the self as a self
from the family, and with the dangers both of overpermissiveness
on the part of the parents and of a too rigorous paternalism which
prevents the child from establishing its independence.

He has dealt in a new way with the religious dimension of
selfhood, that is, with its transcendence over any particular
community or historical configuration, and his study properly
ends with the relation of the self to the religious community as
a community of grace. In all these studies he has drawn on
both significant psychiatric and theological elaborations of basic
problems of the self, of its individuality, of its need for community, and of its need of forgiveness. The volume will therefore
be of tremendous help to all pastors and counselors, and to the
whole Christian community.

R.N.

The Self in Pilgrimage does not provide easy solutions to the
problems of man and society in contemporary life, nor does it set
forth comfortable conclusions about the melioristic tendencies of
history. It is not a moralistic biography nor a case history with
commentary. Neither is it an allegory in the manner of *Pilgrim's
Progress*. It is not a homily. There is no special pleading for either
psychoanalysis or religion: it is not evangelistic, but scientific and
humanistic. It is not a detailed discourse on psychiatry, psychoanalysis, or religion. Neither is it merely another uninspired review
of modern psychology. It is, instead, a work imbued with the
freshness of new observations and original encounters.

Dr. Loomis' book is a penetrating study of stratagems for the
healing of sickness and the maintenance of health, derived from the
combined insights of religion and psychology. It presents a high-
lighted précis of both these disciplines, from Socrates to Freud,

from Philo to Martin Buber, from St. Augustine to Hilaire Belloc and Paul Tillich.

Human nature is illuminated by a realism that ranges from the fumblings of the infant for pleasure to the cruelties of the Buchenwalds in Nazi Germany, the potentialities for evil in South Africa today, and the suicidal skirmishes between free and totalitarian nations in the Cold War. Dr. Loomis shows that free men are not nearly so free as they believe. Not infrequently, they are controlled by their own demons unconsciously projected onto alien societies, classes, and forces.

It would be difficult to imagine a briefer, clearer, more understanding presentation from the psychodynamic standpoint of "The Self in Development" than is to be found in the chapter by that name.

The section entitled "The Self in Communication" is a study of the helping process. It also covers the development of a feeling of identity, the achievement of a sense of reality, and the function of therapy in providing the opportunity for self-fulfillment.

Modern psychodynamics and psychoanalysis illumine the complexities underlying such established modes of behavior as the beliefs, customs, ceremonials, and rituals of religion. Hell, for example, acquires new significance and relevance in Dr. Loomis' writing—in the torment, isolation, separation, lack of communication, loss of identity, and absence of relationship that often characterize human living today.

Socrates said that the unexamined life was not worth living. Dr. Loomis indicates quite as emphatically that the uninvolved, nonparticipating, uncommitted life is a hazard to the self and to society. Through involvement, participation, sharing, burdening oneself, through communication and community, come health and effectiveness. Communion in this way attains new meaning. The Dostoyevskian encounter with evil; the recognition of evil in oneself as well as in others; the capacity for receiving help and for giving it; the quest for new bridges of communication, assistance, and forgiveness—these are the nodal themes in Dr. Loomis' study, important for all students of human behavior and for those involved in the helping process, be it help for sick individuals or for a sick society.

Dr. Loomis' sympathies are broad. He writes with a delicacy, simplicity, kindliness, and humanity, and with such an avoidance of dogmatism and technical jargon that, although he is himself a Protestant, his work should appeal to liberals of all faiths, even to those not formally religious.

He brings new perspectives, broadened backgrounds, and deeper understanding of man and of his social and religious relationships and directions. His thinking is interdisciplinary. He is equally astute as a psychiatrist, as a psychoanalyst, and as a scholar in religion. He brings together modern psychological and psychoanalytic concepts and a basic concern for religious searchings and truths. At a time when there is so much confusion of motivations, so much that is destructive of old organizations and traditional modes of thought, and so much that is threatening to human life on this planet, it is heartening to read of suggestions for survival and fulfillment based on sound psychological thinking, and grounded in historical and religious understanding.

It is particularly fitting that this book should appear so soon after the Joint Commission on Mental Illness and Health has discovered through a national survey[1] that people in personal and emotional stress turn first to the clergy (42 per cent) and only in lesser degree to physicians, psychiatrists, and social agencies. This points up the need for such a book as Dr. Loomis writes. It should be read quite as much by psychiatrists as by the clergy and students of theology. Social workers and intelligent laymen will find it stimulating and helpful. Many people struggling with the conflict between religion and science, and disturbed by the not infrequent antireligious atmosphere of psychoanalysis, will be greatly aided in their thinking. The great institution in which Dr. Loomis works, Union Theological Seminary, New York, is to be congratulated for offering its facilities for the development of such important insights as Dr. Loomis has achieved in his *Pilgrimage*.

Every psychiatrist should find his understanding and competence enlarged by reading Dr. Loomis' discussion of the Greco-Roman and Judaeo-Christian traditions, of the basic functions of religion in society, and of the potential opportunities for religion in a

---

[1] G. Gurin, J. Veroff, and S. Feld, *Americans View Their Mental Health* (New York: Basic Books, Inc., 1960), p. 307.

country where one hundred million of the citizens are church members. And certainly the new and fuller perspective on the troubled, "evil" aspects of human nature presented in this book will enable the clergy (and other helpers of men) to become more understanding and effective.

All this is not meant to imply that there are no matters of controversy contained in this study. They can, however, be used for the purposes of constructive criticism and discussion.

K.E.A.

PREFACE

This book grows out of lectures delivered as the 1958 Auburn Lectures, part of a series given at Union Theological Seminary, New York, since 1947.

The title of the original lecture series, "On Coming to Ourselves in Christ," was suggested by my colleague, Charles R. Stinnette, Associate Professor and Associate Director of the Program in the Interrelations of Psychiatry and Religion. Originally we had planned to deliver the 1958 Auburn Lectures as a joint project, but this plan was later abandoned, and Dr. Stinnette published a portion of the material he had planned as his contribution in his recent book, *Faith, Freedom and Selfhood*.[1]

My own part which eventually became the lecture series has been both condensed in style and expanded in content to make this book. It consisted of five lectures, "The Self in History" (Chapter II), "The Self in Development" (Chapter III), "The Self in Communication" (Chapter IV), "The Self in Community" (Chapter V), and "The Self in Communion" (Chapter VII). The present chapters I and VI ("The Self in Irons" and "The Self in Hell") are newly prepared especially for this volume.

It is not my purpose in this preface to summarize what is to follow or even to state its purpose. That should be clear from the text itself. Rather I should like to express gratitude to those who have influenced and helped me, especially since this help has been so widespread as to have influenced the entire book and does not necessarily evidence itself in any specific reference.

Psychiatrically and psychoanalytically all of my teachers of psychiatry deserve my thanks, especially Robert A. Clark, who

[1] Seabury Press, Greenwich, 1959.

first introduced me to a clinical study of psychiatry and religion, and Kenneth E. Appel, of the Department of Psychiatry at the University of Pennsylvania who epitomized a comprehensive philosophy of psychiatry that is congenial to religion. To the Philadelphia Psychoanalytic Institute, LeRoy M. A. Maeder, my analyst, and Professor Margaret Mahler, who introduced me to the concept of symbiosis (to which I hope I do not do violence in this text), I also want to express appreciation. Chapters III and IV benefited from suggestions and criticisms made by Lucile Meyer, Associate Principal Investigator in Child Psychiatry Research at St. Luke's Hospital, New York City. These same chapters benefited from the opportunity I had of sharing in the teaching of the course on Religion and Human Development with the late Professor Lewis J. Sherrill, the memory of whose spirit and wisdom will always lend inspiration and perspective to my approach to religion and personality development.

I have for years drawn on the thought of Professor Reinhold Niebuhr, especially as it appears in his *Nature and Destiny of Man,* although this is not evident from specific references. With regard to the use of Biblical materials Professor Cyril Blackman of New College, London, and the University of London gave valuable suggestions. My colleagues at Union Theological Seminary, Professor Cyril Richardson and Professor James Muilenburg assisted me in developing my thoughts as set forth in the historical section. Professors Daniel Day Williams and Albert C. Outler, as well as Dr. Gotthard Booth read the entire text and made critical and creative comments at many points. Many of their contributions I have incorporated with thanks; others I have rejected—perhaps at my peril. These words of appreciation need to be accompanied by my acceptance of full responsibility for my work, including its errors.

In the rewriting of my tape-recorded lectures and the preparation of the new chapters I was assisted in a most valuable and gracious manner by Mr. Leonard Gross. He also contributed important suggestions and helpful criticisms and assisted me in enhancing both clarity of design and craftsmanship in execution.

To the Rev. Robert Neale, the Tutor in our Program, special thanks is due for the tedious and accurately performed task of making the index. Three secretaries, Mary Jo Brown, Josephine

Robertson Pearson, and Susannah Masten, made the dictation of portions of the manuscript and its seemingly endless revising more an adventure than a chore. My most intimate colleagues, Professors Charles R. Stinnette and Jack Greenawalt, freed my time from other duties to make study and writing possible.

Finally, no one writes a book without a debt to his family who spares him the time and energy it claims. But I am grateful for more than this, since my wife provided many insights through our shared experiences, as have our children just through growing up in our midst.

E.A.L.

1 ⚙

The Self in Irons

When I was a thoroughly confused young man of twenty-one I came upon a story as decisive for me as any I shall probably ever read. It was a story of a farmer who saw a frightening vision in his barnyard. As he entered, he found the cows peacefully chewing their cuds, the hens clucking to their chicks, a lizard sunning himself without fear. But suddenly there came an incredible transformation. The cows turned into dinosaurs, the chickens to vultures; the lizard became a python, the barnyard a wild and threatening jungle.

The dismaying scene tarried a moment; then it dissolved. Once again the farmer could see his placid cows, the hens and their chicks, the lazy lizard. Ultimately, his terror ebbed. But never again was he to look upon the inhabitants of his barnyard in the way he had before. From that moment on, he was always to wonder which was real, the domestic scene or the primitive wildness.

And I was always to wonder which was the real me, the way I had imagined myself to be or the way I was in depth.

At last, I could begin to know myself.

I thought I had known. I thought I had plumbed my depths. But I was soon to discover that most of the real me had been hiding from reality for years. I had busily engaged in being good and avoiding evil and had not discovered the great wellsprings of both good and evil within myself. I had believed "right," behaved "right," felt the "right" feelings, but the standards of right were not truly mine.

All this suddenly began to change. I realized that if I were

1

something other than what I thought myself to be, then perhaps I was composed of qualities I both saw and despised in others. Could it be that I was selfish? Vindictive? Crude? Lustful? Jealous? Tyrannical? Somehow these possibilities had always been distant and theoretical. Now they were here—and real.

In accepting the possibility of these evil inner threats, however, I came to a discovery that was even more awesome and challenging. I realized that there might be aspects of my strengths I had never known before. While all sorts of social and personal forces are constantly combining to make one turn away from good in oneself, now I suddenly found the strength to admit the possibility that I cared for other people more genuinely than I had given myself credit for. I further admitted that in all probability I had both the intellectual and emotional capacity to help these people about whom I cared. If these aspects of me were true, then I was a better person than I had imagined myself to be.

Of my increased depth and worth I could not, of course, be sure. But of another matter I could be very sure indeed. From that moment on, I knew with utter certainty that if I were ever to become the person I really was in fact, I would have to know and accept both the good and bad in myself. Only by relating the newly discovered virtue and evil in myself could I become myself.

Getting to know myself became a tumultuous adventure. The disquieting and dangerous alternatives led me to a total re-examination of who I was, what I was for, what I must be and do. Some of the decisions growing out of these experiences are still to be vindicated. Some of them may never be. But life could never be the same again.

The impetus to my self-discovery was that story of the man in the barnyard, and I might never have come upon it except for the advice of a professor with whom I was studying at Princeton Theological Seminary. I had been reading, with increasing frustration, the works of Feodor Dostoyevsky. I had complained to my professor, and after many hours of conversation, he had told me to read Dostoyevsky in the realization that he was writing out of his own life—his anguish, his power, his deep inner being. If I could accept this possibility, my professor assured me, I would then meet the author fully with my own being, and we would resonate together.

To "resonate" with another human being is to know that when you speak you are heard by him. The echoes that reverberate to you in his voice are rich with the sounds of your own concern. Similarly, your own voice, echoing back to him, has been affected by what you have heard him say and what you felt that he believed.

My professor was quite right. When I approached Dostoyevsky with a willingness to receive the sounds of his inner life, I heard them. So markedly did I resonate that it became imperative for me to find others who had done so, too. It was the expression of his resonance by the German theologian, Eduard Thurneysen, that gave me what I now see as my particular moment of truth. It was he who asserted that a man who has seen himself in Dostoyevsky's mirror will, like the man in the barnyard, never look the same to himself again.[1]

In a sense, then, my self-discovery began by accident. Most of us, however, are not so fortunate as to benefit from such helpful accidents. Coming to acknowledge possibilities for both good and evil in ourselves is so much of a threat that, lacking the happy accident, too many of us proceed through life in blissful unawareness of who we are. In fear of the unknown we deny our possibility for evil, and commit it unawares. Avoiding responsibility and decision through avoiding inner resources and powers, we evade the challenge to be what we are or can be. We are truly adrift, like a ship in irons.

A ship in irons is as powerless as a shackled human prisoner. It has violated the laws of motion under sail, and has been jailed for its failure. Like a human prisoner, a ship in irons has lost direction, momentum, and control. It can sail neither to port nor to starboard nor straight ahead. It can only stand still or drift backwards.

A self in irons may in part reflect a culture in irons, for the claims and commitments of a culture form a significant dimension of each self that participates in this culture. We in America

---

[1] Eduard Thurneysen, *Dostoyevsky* (4th ed.; Munich: Chr. Kaiser Verlag, 193?.

have advanced far toward a commitment unlike any other in modern times. Our commitment is to the "American dream"—success, adjustment, pleasure, satisfaction, and security, all of which, supposedly, would assure us of a mature society.

Maturity is a useful but difficult word that can mean an end point (the older we get the more mature we are), or a climax (a point toward which we grow until we reach it and then from which we fall away as we approach our second childhood and "grow backwards"); or a concept of appropriate developmental level for our age (living up to our full potentiality). Maturity can mean the opposite of "childishness," which we deem a substitute for age-appropriate behavior. The trouble with the word maturity, however, is that in common usage it has come to mean none of these, but rather a condition that is defined by the conformist's idea of perfectionism—a combination of the previously named "superficial" ingredients of the "happy society."

No single element of the conformist's happy society is necessarily undesirable. But taken together as the be-all and end-all of life, they can be disastrous. They cut us off from the real possibilities of living, simply because they cut us off from the quest for the unique qualities in ourselves that prove each of us to be a creature of God. We force ourselves to deny even that inner restlessness to which Augustine referred when he said, "Thou hast made us for Thyself, O Lord, and our heart is restless until it finds its rest in Thee."[2]

Why do we cut ourselves off from ourselves? Part of the answer, to be sure, is that what impersonal society holds out as good, looks very good indeed. Few of us would turn down a Cadillac. None of us would grumble over a free trip to Bermuda. We like a nice change of clothing, we want our families well fed. We also want the esteem of our peers. To get it, we must succeed on their terms.

It is an important part of self-discovery to participate in the life of our peers, to share in their pleasures and joys, their corporate aims and ideals. But when these goals are not organically linked to the infinitely more substantial pursuit of self-discovery, they become shallow, empty, and blind. They are

[2] *Confessions*, Book I, Part 1.

substitutes that lead us to much knowledge of things, but little knowledge of others and no knowledge of self.

Yet who, when asked to choose, would willingly sacrifice the opportunity to know himself? Who would throw away the hidden treasures that, once mined, might make him a Mozart, an Einstein, or a Schweitzer? Who would want the cures for cancer or schizophrenia to perish in his brain, and thereby deprive himself of the joyous knowledge that in a world of eternal miseries, he had made a difference?

The answer is disturbing. *Most of us* would be afraid to take the needed steps to know ourselves. We refuse to plumb our depths because we fear that in looking for something good we shall also find something horrible: skeletons, hobgoblins, yes, dinosaurs, vultures, and pythons. We fear the emergence of an aspect that will be unacceptable to society, to our peers. We even fear that the very search itself will be condemned, assuming that in questing for the self we would be so selfishly preoccupied as to be insensitive to the needs of others. We know all too well that both religiously and socially such preoccupation is not approved.

But mainly, and most paradoxically, the reason we refuse to search for our inner being is that we fear we shall find something *good*.

We fear good? Americans fear good? This is not easy to believe. It is a fundamental of our social creed that a free society becomes great because its members work to the limits of their intellectual and physical capacity. We give the best we have. When these best efforts are combined, our theory holds, we arrive at the "best" society. The American legend takes nourishment from the log-splitter who became president, the copy boy who became publisher, the attorney who waited on tables in college, and the immigrant who made a million dollars.

The legends are true. But what percentage do their heroes represent of all those who might have done the same thing and didn't? Of those who had the same givens and the same gifts but didn't try? In all probability the heroes are an infinitesimal percentage of the whole.

Why did the vast majority not try? Why did their goodness

remain hidden from them? It was hidden from them because it
was hidden *by* them; they hid their goodness from themselves.
Time after time doctors, in caring for unhappy and unfulfilled
people, discover that the patients were not deficient in potential,
but had concealed their potential from themselves. Instead of
working to full capacity, these people behaved as though they
were inferior, stupid, or unappealing. A child who fears he won't
be liked never finds out how likable he could be. A young girl
who believes she's so unattractive she'll never have a date actually
contributes, by worry, to the poor appearance that fulfills her
fears. The student who is excessively fearful about passing ex-
aminations inhibits his study to such an extent that he does fail.
A woman who fears she cannot love God ultimately flees from
even the thought of Him. These are the kinds of people who find
their way into psychiatrists' offices. They are sick. And it is
their own vitality, the source of their own inner forces, that
is used in the service of the sickness. Even though the sufferer
may blame his own forces, the latter are not sick in themselves.
They are present in the healthiest of us. All of us must wage
this same struggle to confront our own goodness. And all of us,
to some extent, fail.

Why? Why are we afraid to embrace our virtues? Why do we
mask them behind inaccurate estimates and unreasonable fears?
Sometimes we may unconsciously reject our hidden powers because they are linked with impulses that are unacceptable either
to ourselves or to the society in which we set our lives. But the
more common answer is a much simpler one. Basically, we resist
recognition of our assets because, once recognized, they must
be *used*.

For goodness makes claims. It must be expressed. It must be
used. Otherwise, it becomes evil in our hands. Badness is goodness dammed up, just as hell is heaven dammed up. The man
who knows he could help others but helps only himself will
ultimately not be able to live with himself. He will be his own
worst tormentor. The man who knows he could heal people but
is afraid to risk the sacrifice, responsibility, and hardship—as
well as the humbling knowledge that sometimes he will not be

able to heal—is ultimately victimized by his own unfulfillment. The man who will not accept the risk of loving and receiving love will live and die in emptiness.

Literature is full of stories of people who knew they had talent, yet failed to use it. The untold stories are those of the millions of individuals who unconsciously disguised their virtues lest they be obliged to use them—and lost the riches of true living in the process. In this one sense, we human beings are akin to the battery in a flashlight; unused, it corrodes. What we do not use is wasted; what we do not share we cannot keep.

Talents must be invested. Jesus told the story of a man who, departing on a long trip, left certain sums of money, then called "talents," with his three servants. On his return he asked each one what he had done with his money. The first two told their master that they had invested the talents and earned a high return. The third explained that out of fear he had buried his talent in the ground. The master praised the first two servants for their foresight and blamed the third for his sloth. Jesus left us to draw our own conclusions from this story, and these are mine: There *is* a risk in knowing ourselves, just as there is a risk in any investment. We may not like some of the things we find. Or we may not succeed in realizing a return on our talents. But if we permit our fears to be carried to their extreme, we become paralyzed. Afraid to fall, we would never walk. Afraid to love, we would never live.

These fears, as I shall try to show, are largely overestimated. There are ways of coming to know oneself that do not require lasting preoccupation with the self. There are ways of believing in oneself without making oneself the center of the universe. There are ways of accepting oneself without rejecting others. The wildness we might find in our deep selves is not necessarily our damnation. It may be necessary for our salvation. While many of us might think we are happy and complete, few of us ever achieve the kind of fullness that is possible only with and after a thorough-going exploration of our true selves. While a plant does not have to understand what it is to be a plant in order to be one, a human being can never be fully human unless he knows who and what he is. He comes to this understanding by knowing himself not only as angel but as animal. Some of his self-knowledge may not be satisfying, but self-satisfaction is not necessarily the goal or the result of self-searching. The self we ultimately come to know may be far less adequate than the self we would like to imagine we are. *While we may have to sacrifice far more or far less than we dream, in the process of coming to know and accept ourselves for what we are, we often fear most the loss of illusions rather than the true giving up of the self.*

We need such knowledge of our possibilities, unadorned with illusion, before we can ever really live. Certain values of society, and all too frequently of religion, tend to stupefy and anesthetize us. They teach us to avoid pain and sorrow, to deny anxiety. And we gladly, happily embrace this deception. We abdicate our true identity for a superimposed identity. But the superimposition doesn't take. The deception doesn't work. Pain and sorrow and anxiety find us anyway and we, anemic and unprepared, become ill and unhappy. In failing to explore ourselves, we have lost our armor against hardship.

A failure to search for oneself is, in its crippling effects, little better than suicide. It is also a denial of neighbor and of God. We become and remain selves only in relationship; thus the rejection of our deep, true selves is a rejection of our neighbor. We give him short change. And since one of the basic doctrines of the Judaeo-Christian heritage is that we are made in God's image, the denial of our identity—seeing less than the full image of ourselves—is thus to see less than we can of God.

So long as the unrealistic ideals such as the "American Ideal" of success go unchallenged, good minds will fall crippled and unexplored at their feet. Only when we know ourselves can we challenge these crippling myths, for only then can we come to accept ourselves for what we are.

Where can man turn to escape this deception, this vicious circle? To the light of reason advocated by the Greeks? Reason does not illumine the whole man. To the path of obedience followed by the Jews? Conformity cannot guarantee inner obedience. To the light of faith imparted by Christianity? Faith can still be clouded by self-deception. To the light of modern scientific knowledge? Scientism can all too easily dazzle us into complacency, arrogance, and easy self-reliance.

None of these by itself is enough. But taken together—reason, obedience, faith, and science—they may be enough. For along with the general knowledge that science has given us about man has come a special method of understanding self and nature, even in relation to God. It is a method that, linked with religion, may lead us to know our own true and full selves. It is a method arrived at through old faith and new experience. The old faith is the Judaeo-Christian heritage that tells us optimistically about man's potential to do and be good, in spite of its pessimistic reminder of his capacity to do and be bad, and even to turn the good to evil, "the greatest treason." The new method is one that dramatically demonstrates and illumines the old ideas while challenging and testing their application.

Whether we call this method psychoanalysis or psychodynamics or depth psychology, we reflect our comprehension of a new approach to viewing human life, a perspective in depth. This method has laid bare our deeper motives, revealed our latent hostility, and proved how often we deceive ourselves and others, often when we believe we are being our most virtuous selves. But it also discloses our unmined resources for community with one another, for discovery of powers to help and heal ourselves and others; it discloses capacities for perceiving, feeling, and interacting at new levels of effectiveness and love.

Psychoanalysis, by itself, cannot help man achieve a full understanding of himself. It may, however, prove—and prove in our time—to be the catalyst that releases the dormant power in the classical and religious disciplines concerned with mankind. This new science has already helped us to rediscover much that was known in the ancient faiths, but too often petrified by conformity to frozen tradition. Psychoanalysis has laid bare the concrete facts of what has been intuitively known all along, that there is good and bad in man and that life is a continuing fight to unblock good and conquer bad. As Max Scheler has said: "In approximately ten centuries of history, this is the first in which man finds himself completely and utterly 'problematical,' in which he no longer knows what he is and simultaneously *knows that he does not have the answer.*"[3]

For thousands of years, man has looked longingly for himself. Time and again he has come close to discovery, and an occasional seer or saint or scientist has broken through. But for most men the search has all too often been in vain, because too often they fled from their own contradictions. Instead of fleeing, we must face and explore our contradictions in our quest for the self.

Self-knowledge is achieved through a long and difficult pilgrimage. The journey has never been easy, and in some ways it is harder today than ever. Yet today, perhaps more than ever before, man needs to take seriously the pilgrimage toward discovery of himself. His very survival may be determined by his success.

Let not the need for success and the dangers of the journey cause man to despair. There are charts and pilots to guide and guard him on his pilgrimage.

[3] Max Scheler, trans. from the German by Oscar A. Haac, *Philosophical Perspectives* (Boston: Beacon Press, 1958) p. 65. From Chapter IV, "Man and History" (first published in the monthly, *Die Neue Rundschau,* Nov. 1926).

2 ✠

The Self in History

Who are we? Can we ever know? Or are we an abyss whose depths we can never plumb? Is the ancient Greek maxim "Know thyself!" an impossible command? Perhaps yes, perhaps no; in either case, it is not new. A modern biologist, Edmund Sinnott, would answer, "Until man comes to know *himself,* all other knowledge that he gains is incomplete."[1] Man has recognized this truth intuitively ever since thought began; thus the search for the self may properly be considered the oldest treasure hunt in history.

The effort has been constant and great, but in terms of the riches available, the haul has been slight. Most of the treasure still remains hidden. Have we any right to believe that we will now mine these assets, when they have always eluded us before? There are two popular answers to this question: there are those who feel that the methods and insights of modern science will unearth all solutions; others believe that no new knowledge can resolve what history has indicated is irresolvable. Both positions are unrealistic. New insights do give us a right to new optimism. But history should teach us humility. A balance of hope and humility is necessary to the search for the hidden self.

One of the most significant clues in determining how far we have come in the search for the self is to be found in the history of the way in which our ancestors have taken care of each other, or haven't. We ask how they cared for children,

[1] Edmund W. Sinnott, *Matter, Mind and Spirit* (New York: Harper & Brothers, 1957).

11

for the poor, for the sick, for prisoners in peace and in war. And the answers say a great deal about their humanity and inhumanity, their philosophy, their religion—in short, about how they saw man, and, most especially, themselves.

Comparing yourselves with your ancestors, try to imagine yourself in the home of a friend who had just given birth to a child. You ask about her well-being. She tells you she's fine. Then you inquire about her new baby. "Oh," she says, "I took him out last night and left him on a windy hill in the country. We've decided we really can't afford another child." You, or anyone else, would be outraged. You would instantly call the authorities or personally speed to the rescue of the child. Then you would turn to your friend and her obvious problem of mental illness.

Yet, in the ancient world, it was a common practice to dispose of unwanted children by exposing them to the elements and wild beasts. The Greeks, the Romans, the East Indians, and many other ancient peoples practiced this form of infanticide with relatively clear conscience. It was argued that either these infants were not yet real human beings, or their souls would be better off in a more favorable reincarnation, which could be induced by interrupting their present life. In no sense was the act viewed with the horror with which it would be attended today.

The point is not so obvious as it seems.

The concept of the self is interwoven with the history of all mankind's acts, reflections, and feelings. It cuts across many arteries of character. Following its progress is like trying to follow a series of cloverleaf superhighway turnoffs. One discovers that by turning right he has really turned left, because here right means left in terms of the real direction he's after. In this same sense, right does not always mean right; nor does left always mean left as we search for the self. The Greeks, Romans, and East Indians who left their infants to the beasts were highly devoted to the care and nurture of the children they permitted to survive. Thus, to conclude from their practice of infanticide that the ancients were unmitigatedly cruel and were therefore selves of the lowest order would be unfair and inaccurate. The cruelest practices by today's standards appear side by side with examples of humaneness[2] that put modern man to shame.

It is not more difficult to collect examples of humaneness among the ancient peoples than it is to find instances of barbarism in modern man. What *is* difficult is to make sense out of the inconsistencies. Just as we begin to believe that man has learned something about caring for his fellow man we are shocked by his radical departures from this understanding. Just as we begin to hope that he has come to love his fellow man, we see him applying new ingenuity in causing him suffering. The history of the concept of the self, therefore, is no easy course to trace. No single clue is entirely clear, entirely uncontradictory. With these reservations in mind, then, I would like to suggest that there is one clue to the history of selfhood that, even allowing for inconsistencies, is perhaps more revealing than others. *This clue is man's conception of God.*

Man's image of God and his image of himself are somehow always linked together. "In the history of human thought," notes Professor Casserley, Special Chaplain to graduate students and faculty of the University of Chicago, "the doctrine of God and the doctrine of man rise and fall together. The more profound our sense of the reality and meaning of divinity, the more vivid our apprehension of the unique status and dignity of human personality."[3] Man's image of God is not, however, a simple

---

[2] The pagans and their gods were capable of remarkable kindness to strangers and enemies. For example, in Homer's *Odyssey,* Ulysses, lost and alone, comes upon a strange island. There a young girl offers to lead him to her king and queen. This is dangerous for Ulysses because the people of this island are belligerent. But the young girl, who represents Athena the goddess of reason and balance, tells Ulysses exactly what to do to be safe.

In the *Iliad,* Achilles, full of vengeance toward Hector, kills him in battle and desecrates his corpse by dragging it over the ground, contrary to all moral rightness. But when Hector's father comes to Achilles and mourns his loss, the two men weep together, and together arrange a funeral for Hector. Cf. Walter F. Otto, *Homeric Gods* (New York: Pantheon Books, 1954), pp. 6-7, 259-60.

[3] J. V. Langmead Casserley, *The Christian in Philosophy* (New York: Charles Scribner's Sons, 1951).

subject to investigate. We must, first of all, ask *which* of man's
Gods we are studying.

For every man there are at least three gods: God as He really
is; God as his group sees Him; and God as developed within the
mind of the individual. About the first God, a psychiatrist can
say nothing as psychiatrist; theologians and philosophers themselves are divided in their opinions whether God can be known
as He actually is in Himself,[4] and the theories about just Who
or What He is are varied. About man's second God, much has
been said. Doctrines about this God have been believed and
promulgated by religious communities and scholars from ancient
times. It is man's third concept of God that inhibits or modifies
each person's acceptance of the God of his church. Whatever
God is in Himself, whatever He may be to each church, each
man's conception of God is to a significant extent the unwitting
work of man himself. The personality or impersonality man as-
cribes to God is almost always a reflection of the fullness or
emptiness of his own inner being.

For at some time in his life each individual begins to develop
his private picture of God.

This private God may be a reflection of a parent. He may
be what the parent is really like, or what the child wishes the
parent were like, or even what the child fears the parent is like.

This private God may be a reflection of the need of the child
or adult. If the need is for power, then God may assume a powerful countenance. If the need is for goodness, then God may be
perfect. If the need is for punishment, then God will be vindictive.

This private God may even be a reflection of the community.
If the community is seen by the child as hostile, his God may
reflect either the community's hostility or the child's compensatory wish for protection.

As children grow up, they modify their childish notions of
God to conform more and more with the ideas of their religious

---

[4] Daniel Day Williams, professor of theology at Union Theological Seminary, correctly submits that properly and by definition a *theologian* has
implicit or explicit assumptions about the possibility of understanding God.
Philosophers may not. I think, however, that there are some theologians
who would not fit into this former category.

community. But some remnants of the private God-image always remain, coloring and modifying the adult faith.

There are, it need hardly be added, many people capable of achieving a philosophical or theological vision of God. But we all too rarely find the mature religious mind that is capable of distinguishing between God Himself and the projection of the images within the self onto God. For most of us these two Gods are always confused and confounded. To a great extent our ideas and feelings toward God continue to reflect our inner expectations and experiences—and thus the historical visions of God remain invaluable clues to the visions of the self.

Because man's image of God reflects his vision of himself, the *development* of the image, it follows, is a reflection of the development of the self. It is much more. It is a history of man's incessant attempts to bury aspects of himself he has not dared to confront. It is also a proof that when man makes such attempts, he fails. No fundamental aspect of human personality—or its interaction with God or man—can ever be successfully suppressed. In demonstration of this we have examples from the religious history of the Greeks, the Jews, the Eastern faiths and, as we shall see, the Christian Church, the currents on which we move today. These examples constitute only fragments of the history of religion and man. In no sense are they to be considered a comprehensive survey of man's view of his own nature. Nevertheless, they represent significant landmarks of man's attempt at self-disguise—and its consequences.

Most ancient Greeks were dominated by a popular, superstitious religion. A more esoteric philosophical faith had a smaller number of followers. The larger group pictured a world of major and minor deities who inhabited Mount Olympus, visiting their whims and fancies upon mortal man who dwelt on the plains below. These gods could transform themselves into men, and men into animals or plants. They could influence battles by changing the weather or by confusing the minds of armies. They could engage in treachery or trickery. They represented in many ways orgiastic gods of the underworld, requiring and representing neither righteousness, obedience, reason, nor order. These gods could sometimes be placated by sacrifice, but at other times they ran roughshod over helpless man.

On the other hand, the small band of Greek philosophers had thoughts of God that reached incomparably high degrees of virtue, clarity, and order. In fact, these God-ideas became so rarified and orderly—perhaps as a reaction against the undisciplined and scandalous popular deities—that they tended to sound (at least to us today) sterile, impersonal, and abstract.

The fusion of the superstitious, popular religion with the philosophical ideas produced a contradiction in man's concept of God. It also confused man's idea of himself. Instead of seeing himself as one, he tended to the view that he consisted of two separate and distinct parts, one a rambunctious body, the other a rational soul. The rambunctious nature, having to do with man's emotions, desires, and affections, was regarded as low and base. Particularly low and base were the sexual functions—because of the insistent claims they could make on man and the ease with which they could overcome his higher rational nature. The Greek philosophers' tendency to devaluate and depreciate the body and its functions was one origin of the ambiguous attitude toward sex that appears today in much of Western religion; it remains one of Christianity's most unfortunate borrowings from antiquity.

The pagans were correct in reporting that man had at least two sides to himself; and polytheism, the belief in more than one god, could accurately represent this fact. But just as polytheism cannot bring the gods together, so the Greeks failed to bring man's two sides together.

As a consequence of this philosophical dualism, the rejected side of man emerged with an actually heightened intensity in the form of orgiastic religious cults, the most famous of which was the Dionysian. Here the masses worshiped the god of wine through abandon to his products, and the physical and emotional ecstasies thus induced gave expression to that which man had sought to hide.

An even greater extreme of splitting apart the self is seen in some of the Eastern religions. They, too, accurately revealed man's uncertainty of himself as a whole being. These religions thought of God as the One into whom each individual must merge and thereby lose his unvalued personal identity. For some of the more enlightened this merger represented not so much a loss of the self as an expansion of the lightly regarded self into the divine *superself*. For many, however, becoming part of God meant the complete loss of selfhood. God, therefore, was seen as the enemy of the individual self, for it was He in whom the self was to be dissolved.

Pagan religions separated man's spirit from his body; for many Indians, this cleavage was brought about by allowing the body to perish out of unconcern, or manipulating it through yogic exercises into a vessel having no claims of its own but totally commanded by the soul and sacrificed to the soul's salvation. To this day, much of East Indian culture finds it difficult to develop enthusiasm for physical or public health and for certain types of humanitarian concern that seem indispensable to Western man.

But the Indians could not abandon the body altogether; it was too compelling in its claims. First of all, they demonstrated their respect for the body through their emphasis on nonviolence toward animals. Second, like the Greeks, they managed to find in their pantheon of deities, representations of every human passion and vice. Krishna was a god who seduced hundreds of maidens. Prajāpati and Dhātri procreated millions of offspring. Durge and Kali demanded bloody sacrifices. Shiva delighted in the destruction of life. Ganeca was behind hosts of frightening demons. Each of these gods represented deep and ubiquitous drives in both man and nature, yet each was a different god. And like the gods, the self remained fragmented.

Coming to the Hebrews, we find for the first time in a persisting religion an unclouded statement that God is One. Although up to the time of Second Isaiah even the Hebrews were monolatrists, seeing God as King over lesser gods, since then their call, "Hear, O Israel: the Lord our God, the Lord is one," (Deuteronomy 6:4) has resounded unambiguously down the centuries.

To the extent that Old Testament religion was truly monotheistic and God was One for the Hebrews, so the Hebrews were one to themselves. Man's basic psychosomatic unity was real to the Hebrew both in religion and in everyday life; he saw his body and spirit as a unit—not as separate parts hooked together.

One of the accounts of creation suggests that this unity had been built into man from the outset. In Genesis 2:7 we find: ". . . the Lord God formed man of dust from the ground, and breathed into his nostrils the breath of life; and man became a living being."

One needs only to read the Psalms to feel the passion with which he perceived the oneness of his body and spirit:

> my eye is wasted from grief,
> my soul and my body also.
> For my life is spent with sorrow, and my years with sighing;
> my strength fails because of my misery,
> and my bones waste away.   [Psalm 31, RSV]

> O Lord, rebuke me not in thy anger,
>   nor chasten me in thy wrath!
> For thy arrows have sunk into me,
>   and thy hand has come down on me.
> There is no soundness in my flesh
>   because of thy indignation;
> there is no health in my bones
>   because of my sin.
> For my iniquities have gone over my head;
>   they weigh like a burden too heavy for me.
> My wounds grow foul and fester
>   because of my foolishness,
> I am utterly bowed down and prostrate;
>   all the day I go about mourning.
> For my loins are filled with burning,
>   and there is no soundness in my flesh.
> I am utterly spent and crushed;
>   I groan because of the tumult of my heart.
> Lord, all my longing is known to thee,
>   my sighing is not hidden from thee.   [Psalm 38, RSV]

The organic intimacy of the creator God with man's body is further illustrated in Psalm 139:

> For thou didst form my inward parts,
>   thou didst knit me together in my mother's womb.
> I praise thee, for thou art fearful and wonderful.
>   Wonderful are thy works!

> Thou knowest me right well;
> > my frame was not hidden from thee,
> when I was being made in secret,
> > intricately wrought in the depths of the earth.

For centuries man has viewed himself through the lenses supplied by the Greeks. Through one lens the Greeks saw man as physical and as part of nature. Through the other they—and others after them—saw man as pure and nonphysical spirit. Their image of man was therefore split—just as though they had been looking through two separate telescopes instead of one pair of binoculars. Man's physical side remained related solely to nature; his spiritual side solely to philosophy or God. What the Hebrews perceived was that man is a unity; his physical and spiritual natures are one. Instead of the mind being a representation of abstract spirit, and the body a representation of matter in general, each living being is indivisible. The body is spiritual; and the spirit is concrete. This kind of thinking, so alien to classical and medieval—even modern—thinking, can now be rediscovered in the Old Testament as a great but long lost heritage from the ancient Hebrews.[5]

Perhaps no one knows or ever will know exactly how and why and when the nomadic Semitic tribes came to perceive this basic truth of man's nature. What we do know is that in early biblical times we come upon a character such as Abraham to whom God revealed Himself—initially as the One who demanded the sacrifice of Abraham's only son. But when Abraham's obedience was seen, God miraculously rescued the lad from the sacrificial knife and supplied in his stead a ram. This God of the

[5] Professor Johannes Pedersen of Copenhagen declares, "The Israelite has no independent term for will as we understand the word. He does not recognize the will as an independent feature or force of the soul. . . . The soul is totality . . . the will is the whole of the tendency of the soul." Cf. Johannes Pedersen, *Israel: Its Life and Culture* (London: Oxford University Press, 1926), Vol. I, Parts 1-2, p. 103.

Professor James Muilenburg of Union Theological Seminary in New York points out that for the Hebrew, the "living person is one and indivisible." (Personal communication.) In contrast with the tendency toward generality and abstraction, thinking, to the Hebrew, was concrete. dramatic, and holistic.

Hebrews could combine in Himself the contraries that other faiths had to split into multiple deities.

The Hebrews maintained that God was Creator and Sustainer of the universe and of the life of each man—and that each man was made in His image. Yet somehow even the Hebrews could not always live by this image of God. In time they refused to accept this image and they revolted against its claims. As reflected in the Apocryphal writings, they developed demons to whom they ascribed the unacceptable in themselves as well as their God.[6]

The appearance of Christ, Christians believe, gave to men a reminder both of who God is and who *they* are. If to be himself man must express God's image, then here, for the first time, was God in the flesh. Suddenly man no longer had to guess about God's image. He could see God's image. He could see

---

[6] The Hebrew and Greek positions seem poles apart in theory. In practice, both of them tended to be modified by the existence of the other, and most real persons combined both outlooks and attitudes. One intermediate position—that of the Hellenistic-Jewish philosophers—served as a bridge between the Greek and Hebrew positions as well as to the Christian philosophical beginnings. The most noteworthy representative, Philo of Alexandria, a contemporary of Jesus, combined the Hebrew philosophic tradition with aspects of Platonic and Stoic philosophy. He saw the universe as populated with spirits, but depreciated nature in favor of reason rather than seeing nature itself as worthy of scientific inquiry, as would the Greeks. As the late Gregory Zilboorg pointed out, "The existence of man as man was thought to be due to an original moral fall and original sin." (Cf. Gregory Zilboorg and George W. Henry, *History of Medical Psychology* [New York: Norton, 1941], pp. 96-97). It was as if man had to deplore his own creation—an attitude implying that man's salvation depends on his ceasing to be a created human being. It is as if there were something wrong with being human.

In the atmosphere of "dying classicism" of Philo's time, man's body was depreciated, his spirit was exalted, and his personality was ignored. Any mental disorder was viewed as either spiritual or somatic. There was room for neither psychology nor psychosomatic medicine. Man had lost sight of himself as a holistic being and had lost sight of his God as being relevant to his human or bodily existence. (Professor Albert C. Outler questions to what extent it is altogether fair to single out Philo as the representative whipping boy in the scourging of antiholism. He calls our attention to the fact that not only Philo, a Hellenistic Jew [20 B.C. to A.D. 54] but also St. Paul, a Christian convert from Judaism, could depreciate the "body" and "flesh and blood." [Compare ". . . flesh and blood cannot inherit the kingdom of heaven . . ." I Corinthians 15:50, RSV. And ". . . we know that while we are at home in the body we are away from the Lord . . ." II Corinthians 5:6, RSV.])

what God did, know what He felt; understand what God wished
for man's true self to be. Christ was alive and human. He shared.
He gave. He loved. He wept. He became outraged at injustice.
He was impatient with stupidity, scathing toward hypocrisy.

His appearance to the Jews was both a fulfillment and a
scandal. For those to whom he came to mean the long expected
Messiah, he seemed to offer hope of deliverance of Jerusalem
and Israel from the Roman captivity. This was not Jesus' mission.
These expectations came to nought, and these Jews were disillu-
sioned and they resented both Jesus and their own gullibility.

Others saw his very tendency to imply a new interpretation of
the law and the prophets as blasphemous. Furthermore, the Jews
had been faithful in their avoidance of images or idols of their
God and they were suspicious of, indeed outraged at, any sug-
gestion of a visible manifestation of deity in a man. Incarnation
was a scandal too reminiscent of the pagan demigods which they
had successfully rejected.

But for the followers of Jesus, all this was evaluated as not
simply the behavior of another prophet who was especially good,
especially godly, and especially human. Rather, they saw Jesus
as a revelation, a disclosure, indeed the one full and genuine incarnation—a coming in the flesh—of the God of the Hebrews,
the God of the Old Testament.[7]

Jesus was so remarkable that he was unendurable, and he had
to be crucified. His healings might be helpful and his teachings
thought-provoking, but this incarnational behavior had come "too
close to home." It was too reminiscent of the incarnational themes
of rival pagan mystery cults.

The mystery of this person was not cleared up in the thirty-

---

[7] "The God of the Bible is not an ineffable One, a remote and lofty Absolute, who is searched out by an abstruse philosophical method which inevitably falls short of Him, and is found only rarely in the bliss of mystical
absorption and ecstasy. The God of the Bible is the active creator-God
who reveals Himself in events—in the history of Israel and the biography of
Jesus—as Person, Purpose, and Will. The Bible speaks of Him in terms of
confident affirmation, telling of His Purpose, His Providence, His Justice,
His Wrath, and His Love. He has shown Himself to us in Jesus, so that
'whoever has seen Jesus has seen the Father,' because Jesus is 'the image of
the invisible God!' " J. V. Langmead Casserley, *The Christian in Philosophy*,
p. 38.

odd years he dwelt as a man on this earth in a remote province of the Roman Empire. He was obviously a Jew, and so far as we can tell, received no special training other than that of the ordinary rabbi of his time. Yet he was a man who "spoke with authority," whom "the common people heard gladly." That he healed the sick and performed miracles did not really distinguish him from the earlier prophets or from rabbis before, during, and after his time. That he preached judgment on the outwardly religious who were inwardly corrupt was directly in the line of the greater prophets of Israel. That he preached obedience out of love, and forgiveness out of grace rather than mechanical legalism was further consistent with his prophetic predecessors.

It was also nothing new that a prophet's life should be in jeopardy. This, too, was in the main line of Jewish tradition. The painful truth is rarely welcomed with open arms.

Yet a few even before his death, and multitudes after it, came to believe that Jesus was unique. He demanded explaining.

Was he just the best that humankind could produce, the finest fruit of human evolution and development? Was he simply a manifestation of Deity who took on himself temporarily an appearance of human form? Did he have one nature or two? Could he really have sinned? And if not, could he therefore have truly been tempted, even as man is tempted? Did he know who he was from the beginning? Did he have to discover it, and if so, how? Through foreknowledge? Special revelation from God? Or was it by interaction with other persons?

These questions and many more occupied six centuries of Christological conflict and debate.[8] Out of the dedicated and difficult struggles of the first three of these centuries grew a magnificent synthesis, the implications of which have only begun to be realized.

The central theme of this synthesis is that of unity: the combining into an organic union of what seemed to be otherwise contradictory elements. In Christ—one person—was true man-

_____

[8] Professor Outler reminds us that the Christological conflicts began with the Gnostic struggle in the second century and raged on until the aftermath of the Iconoclastic controversy in the closing decades of the eighth century. (Personal communication.)

hood and true divinity. These elements came into dynamic tension and relationship around the central figure who could combine and relate in himself both time and eternity. He was a creature of time, was born, grew up, and died, but he was and is also in and of God, outside the constrictions of time and space.

Only after the synthesizers had successfully formulated a conception of the personality of Jesus did man at last develop a full-fledged idea of the human person. Only after Christ came could man awake from his earlier unawareness of himself as a person. It was as though the second Adam (Christ) revealed to man the meaning of being a son of the first. It was as though God had to send Christ to show us who we were as well as who He was. *Only through learning who He was could we have begun to learn who we are.*

Who was He? Even the image of man in the Jesus of the Bible and the Church is not the full human self as it must be known by us. We know little or nothing of His personality development as a child, a youth, or an adult. The aspects of his life that the psychiatrist would so dearly love to understand are unknown. His sexual and social development, his family life, his loves and hates, his occupation and his recreation are hidden. We miss most of the crucial aspects of what today we would demand in a well-rounded picture of human nature and life.

Theologians have struggled with the problem of Christ's sexuality. Some have turned to apocryphal accounts of a romance. Others have approached the problem by insisting that if Christ's maleness had been stressed, he would have been less than a perfect model for women. Some scholars have even reverted to the old Greek rejection of sexuality, and suggested that Christ did indeed represent an asexual ideal.

These explanations are escapes. We cannot manufacture the missing links; we can only conjecture. What is clear is that for the Early Church it was not considered important to conserve or teach details of Christ's human life, except those that had direct bearing on salvation. The concerns of the Early Church so ignored the human life of Christ that in concrete terms he is portrayed as a most attenuated version of a concrete human being. Therefore we should be hesitant in representing this version to our youth as the epitome of perfect manhood. *He may well have been perfect.* And this is the faith of Christendom. But we do not have the picture of *all* aspects of his life—and to present such an emasculated image is to ask for emasculated copies in those for whom the imitation of Christ is practiced.

So while at last man had an idea of God that did justice to God as well as to his relation to God, his creaturehood, his sin, and his salvation, this was not enough. The image of Jesus remained a picture to be associated with divinity and not with man himself. Instead of being able to appropriate Jesus' oneness, man was assailed by a long series of theological contradictions. He was told that he was the victim of original sin and therefore inevitably and unavoidably sinful—and that he was also the possessor of free will. Man was told that God was both benevolent and wrathful; that salvation was both a free gift and a reward for holy works. True as these seemingly paradoxical statements may have been, they were too much for man.[9] Even though he might have been able to stretch his intellect to encompass the doctrines, even though he might have confessed his faith with a loud voice, his understanding of both his God and himself was far afield from his daily life. The truth had been discovered, but it had scarcely been appropriated.

It is one thing to know about the truth; it is another to make use of it. If man for once had the opportunity of discovering his own unity through the model of Christ's, he did not take advantage of the opportunity. He never really has.

Instead of confronting the future with all of himself, man has waged a divided battle. He has simply refused to admit the contradictions in himself or allowed them to work to his own benefit. He has constantly suppressed whatever side of himself he viewed with disfavor. But what happens when man permits one aspect of himself to dominate the other? The subdued element becomes a saboteur; ultimately it erupts. This process is one of the great motifs of history. One recognizes the inescapable similari-

---

[9] In a sense, this confusion was necessary for the survival of the Church. It could not attack every evil of the world and of itself at once. That the Church did survive suggests that some of the priorities were soundly selected. For the task of integration was mammoth.

ties between modern events and one of the greatest outpourings of evil in history—the age of witch-hunting.

This period, which extended from the late Middle Ages through the Renaissance and Reformation and covered about five centuries, is perhaps the most striking historical example that extreme good and extreme evil can exist side by side. The age of witch-hunting was a period of great theological and philosophical thought, of great artistic and creative advance. It was the age of Michelangelo, Dante, Vivaldi, Erasmus, Newton, Calvin, and Luther. But it was also a period of one of the most fantastic eruptions of the underworld in all of history.

The attempt to influence the powers of nature or the will of God by human efforts is as old as religion itself. In a sense it is the underside of religion, the unacceptable poor relation of the respectable faiths. Black magic always is found hanging somewhere around the fringes of white. In biblical literature, there is always someone tagging after every prophet, beseeching him to use his power for personal pleasure or gain.

Around the truest truths of high religion there is always the fringe of quasi-religious, quasi-pagan, quasi-magical practices. Some have been tolerated, even temporarily encouraged by the churches in one interest or another. But something different happened in the great witch-hunts of the Middle Ages. It was as if the kingdom of evil was tired of playing second best and now demanded primary allegiance. It was as if the whole world suddenly took sides: there were those who would worship Satan and those who would fight him and his worshipers. Ironically, as the excitement of the great conflict grew, more and more attention was paid to Satan, and he became more and more real to the medieval world. In effect, his enemies gave him reality.

The witchcraft of the Middle Ages was believed in not only by the remnants of the "Old Religion," which had persisted underground in western Europe despite the mass Christianizing of the Franks and the Germanic tribes. It also became an article of faith for the Church, so that theologians and philosophers as diverse as Pope Innocent VIII, Luther, Calvin, John Wesley, John Knox, and Francis Bacon considered the denial of the validity of witchcraft an evil tantamount to rejection of the faith.

The nightmare era of witchcraft brought out the worst in man, society, and religion. There have been other periods in which witches were believed in but left alone; the popular imagination did not dwell on them to the point of preoccupation. Rather, witches existed at the level of superstition, convenient targets for casual blame, benevolently tolerated, necessary evils. But with the furor of the witch hunts, the power of suspicion became overwhelming. Each man doubted his neighbor, and the contagion of doubt seemed to infiltrate the entire Western world, festering into deep abscesses that could only be healed by eruption. Witchcraft became an unconscionably expensive luxury.

As the late English poet and lay theologian, Charles Williams, put it, once the imagination was focused on the prisoner or suspect, he gave

form and validity to the imagination. It was the pretty young woman in the next house, the ascetic priest of the parish, the dignified wife of the town-councillor, the idiot son of the poor couple in the hovel, the old market-woman with the power of invective, the wandering pedlar, the learned scholar, at whom men and women looked; whom . . . they imagined doing this and the other—talking to the tall black, running upstairs to a materializing lover, dancing, kissing, blaspheming. They felt the sudden unexpected moments when anything or anyone —one's wife, one's friend, one's neighbour—*might* be something else, disguised and malicious.

. . . It needs but for a moment to contemplate another human being with that possibility in mind, in the street or in the train or the house to understand what happened. Add the temptation, the fever, the panic fear; add the longing—so universal though so generally denied nowadays—for hate, for anger, for destruction. The moment of doubt, of horror, of enjoyment of the thrill, resolved itself into belief instead of into disbelief. . . .[10]

Estimates vary as to how many persons went to the rack, the gibbet, and the stake. It has been reckoned that hundreds of thousands, perhaps millions met death through such madness.

One witch finder alone, Williams notes, boasted of some seven hundred executions, and in one city, Berne, there were nine hundred in ten years. Five thousand were burned in Alsace in one

[10] Charles Williams, *Witchcraft* (New York: Meridian Books, Inc., 1959), pp. 168-69.

twenty-year period. While execution was usually by burning, it was often preceded by beheading, strangling, or mutilation. "Pain," writes Williams, "brought the human spirit to its last point of mortal existence; there, in its nakedness, it was asked and answered the question. . . . But now the idea of the solemn rarity of the agony was lost; the pain became popular, and monotonous, and irrelevant."[11]

Whatever the estimates, the literature available makes it perfectly clear that demonology was a major motif of the Western world from the thirteenth through the eighteenth centuries. Every manifestation of treason, heresy, licentiousness, original thought, and even fresh piety, was suspected of being devil-inspired. So auspicious was the movement that in 1484 the Pope accepted the handbook of torture and inquisition propounded by the two German Dominican monks, Sprenger and Kraemer, as the official text of a devil-conscious era. One of the most horrible books of all time, it was called the *Malleus Maleficarum,* or the *Witches' Hammer.* This book, which had implicit approval of Protestants as well as Catholics for centuries, is a nightmare of self-disclosure of the human psyche of the Middle Ages and perhaps of all time. It is marked by three major ideas: first, evil comes from the devil, and man is his accomplice; second, women are the devil's principal collaborators in the undermining of sanctity, virtue, and salvation; and third, torture may be necessary and desirable to "assist" man in telling the truth and to disclose the satanic origin of the unacceptable in our neighbor.

The book became a mighty instrument. Suddenly almost anything that human beings could do or imagine could be ascribed by the populace to the Devil. And those who were alleged to be possessed by him in turn could be condemned and annihilated.

Witchcraft was an attack on the body, on the wholeness of man. It was also an attack upon the sexual functions of men and women—especially women. Allegations against the alleged witches and sorcerers are all too rich in sexual accusations for this to be overlooked. Witches were especially blamed for what we today would call impotence and sterility, and to a lesser degree for

[11] *Ibid.,* p. 178.

frigidity and abortion. What is most striking is the emphasis on the woman's power to undermine man's potency.

In the trials of witches, the collective hate for women of many millenniums suddenly reached a climax. It was taught on the one hand that witches sought and enjoyed sexual congress with devils or devil-created beings called *incubi*. While theologically it was not believed that such beings actually existed, for the popular mind they were as real as the angels and devils themselves. These incubi were blamed for taking part in lewd sexual activities with both the witches and certain innocent female victims. Other devil-inspired creatures called *succubi* were supposed to steal into the beds of men, rouse them sexually during their sleep and steal their sperm, which later was used for immoral purposes.

In substance, every natural human emotion was now given a demonic explanation. Not only were the demons and witches supposed to stimulate and gratify sexually in immoral ways, they were also alleged to interfere with "normal sexual satisfaction," in disrupting marriages and tempting spouses to infidelity.

Catholic and Protestant theologians alike supported the witch hunts. As Charles Williams points out, "The fires of Tyrol were answered by the fires of Geneva," and "if our fathers erred, they erred all together. Catholic and Reformed disputed about heaven; they almost made a pact over Hell."[12]

The authorities who used the *Malleus* to torture an era were the same authorities who were elsewhere proclaiming God's love. They were the Church. They were the Inquisition. They were and are the historical proof that men recognized both good and evil in themselves and in God. With this manifesto in their hands, thousands of exorcists and inquisitors went forth to do battle with the devil and his hosts, and with one another.[13] Now it became not only legal but mandatory to expose, inform, torture,

---

[12] *Ibid.*, p. 177.

[13] The *Malleus* itself is its own best critic, but the descriptions of the behavior of the representatives of the Church and the State, the common man and the aristocracy, the sane and the insane, is dramatically and tragically set forth in accounts of this period, examples of which are included in Zilboorg and Henry's *History of Medical Psychology,* Walter Bromberg's *Man above Humanity,* Charles Williams' *Witchcraft* and Aldous Huxley's *The Devils of Loudun.*

and kill; over three centuries of victims were claimed (and we may count among them the persecutors) before the devil retired —or more properly, before the mad world changed its demonology.

A few voices spoke out against the blindness, the cruelty, and the impiety of this assault upon mankind. Some church-operated hospitals cared for the mentally ill. A Franciscan monk, Bartholomeus Anglicus, wrote a humane and sensitive document on the care of the insane in 1275, even as about him raged the hysteria of witchcraft. All during this period there existed a group of monks, the Order of the Holy Trinity, made up of men willing to give themselves as substitutes for slaves and galley prisoners. Other orders were dedicated to the care of the sick, the poor, the aged, the orphans.

Friedrich von Spee, a Jesuit (whose hair was prematurely whitened by horrors he had seen committed upon the condemned) protested that "some judges and Inquisitors made money out of the trials."

A psychiatrist, Johannes Weyer, pointed out the presence of mental illness in many of the accused and did much to encourage a demand for exact proof that ultimately affected the entire legal system of Europe. To do justice to them, it must be admitted that on matters of witchcraft, the directors of the Inquisition were the leaders of that demand.

The Church was not always blind to the dangers of a popular witch hysteria. In fact, as early as the tenth century, Bishop Regino of the Diocese of Prum collected a group of Rules on Witchcraft which he attributed (probably incorrectly) to the Council, or Synod of Ancyra. This collection was taken up by Gratian in his *Decretum* about the year 1140 and found its place in the compilation under the title, *canon Episcopi*. The statement there pointed out that only God has power, and the witches only do in fantasy what they claim miraculously to do in their bodies. Only the Creator can make or transform things. And here the first chapter of the Gospel of St. John is invoked: "All things were made by Him, and without Him was not anything that was made."

"This was the great achievement of the 'quality of disbelief,' " Charles Williams notes. "Unfortunately, the great vision of the

One Mover could not be adequately communicated to all the men and women of Europe. The Church, three centuries after, went back on its own law."[14]

This "quality of disbelief" constitutes a necessary corrective to all gullibility, superstition, and, in the best sense, heresy. There is a sense in which doubt is a necessary safeguard to faith, and it was the loss of this quality of doubt—honest, inquiring skepticism—that contributed so greatly to the loosing of the forces of destruction during the centuries of the witch trials.

The few merciful voices mentioned above risked torture, death, and excommunication by gently raising the question, "Could the alleged victims of the Devil be mentally ill?" or could their "confessions," obtained under torture, be forced fantasies rather than fact? But while these groups worked to overcome evils, wrong was on the throne and power was in its hands.

How was it that through Christ man had finally come to the opportunity to know himself, and then kicked the opportunity away with a viciousness that was anathema to Christian love? How is it that man continues to do the same today? It would take a strange being to perpetuate this delusion, and man is that strange being. Worshiping a perfect God, he demands perfection in himself as well as in his God. And the Devil is born. Man has never been able to accept the pain of contradiction. He cannot see that the barnyard animals and the wild animals are really the same animals. What caused these Christians to create such black chapters in church history? Simply their everlasting humanness. They shared with their ancestors the very same emotions and hungers: lust and hate, fear and guilt, selfishness and domination, pride and unconcern.

They feared God. His unattainable perfection judged their sinfulness. His omniscient vision left them no hiding place. His omnipotence and wrath doomed them to eternal torment.

They feared their own beings. Their natural vitality seemed like insatiable lust. Their self-transcendent vision seemed like Promethean arrogance. Their perpetual task of binding contradictions seemed an impossible assignment—and so they fled.

They felt guilty. From the dawn of time, man has expected that

14 *Op. cit.,* pp. 72-75.

an eye would be required for an eye, a tooth for a tooth. Like all men before them, the people who induced and endured the Inquisition felt guilty about their acts, their fantasies, and their feelings. Their fantasies they blocked out. Their feelings they concealed, even from themselves. But their acts were public and could not be hidden from God or man.

And so, feeling guilty, they had to have someone to blame. They projected their guilt onto the Devil.

But even the Devil was not enough. They had to make devils of each other.

Nowhere is the projection outward of the hell within so dramatically shown in a religious context as in the Inquisition, whose attacks on heretics and lunatics seemed to be interchangeable. Protestant continuity of the persecution of witches persisted almost unabated, making this common enemy, the witch, at least one point of contact between the Roman and the Reformed. All accounts point to a massive fear and hate reaction in the oppressor and to a curious complicity in the oppressed. They actually, like fanatical false martyrs, sought and provoked their own persecution. It could almost be said that the more dire the threats against, and the punishments for, witchcraft, the more it flourished, the more deluded women and men gave themselves over to its illusion, the more even former persecutors became themselves susceptible to its ravages. In contrast with a *folie a deux* or *trois* (a "contagious" insanity of two or three persons) it became a madness of millions.

It is important that the world remember these outrages against the human spirit, these travesties on the divine will, these temptations to mass ideology, not only as a lesson in history, but as sobering insight on reality. For the delusions continue today. Witchcraft of the Middle Ages is no worse than Nazi persecution of the Jews or contemporary purges of men whose thinking does not conform, or whose skin or faith is not acceptable. Buchenwald, Hiroshima, Budapest, Little Rock, and Johannesburg are addenda to the *Witches' Hammer*.

What seems to have been assumed across the centuries is that what we don't know won't hurt us, particularly when it has to do with our own selves. Even the Church has fallen prey to man's self-defeating tendency to push out of awareness that which displeases him. Banished to the underworld, his unacceptable impulses and wishes and strivings rise again and again in ever-new disguises. More often than not we imagine these subversives to be foreigners, whereupon we can blame others for their intrusion. Little do we guess that they are our own chickens coming home to roost, our own exiled children returning as our enemies.

The excuse for the Middle Ages was their ignorance of psychodynamics and the wide variety of manifestations of mental illness. They did not have the "quality of disbelief" that our modern generation possesses. We have a skepticism that saves us from *witches*. But in our own time our very skepticism is reserved for the superstitions of other persons and other times. Ironically, we lack the quality of disbelief in relation to our own political, ethical, and scientific positions. We can laugh at the witches of others but we can't recognize our own.

If it is the nature of creaturehood to be in conflict, it is also true that this conflict is something against which man continually fights. Could he be asking to return to a source or condition he no longer remembers, or asking to transcend the present and take refuge in the beyond? As Gotthard Booth has pointed out, with all the new methods we have developed for approaching the self, we have also acquired new methods for disguising the self behind the miracles of science, technology, and human engineering.[15]

Today we have two unprecedented if unusual allies we have never had before to tear away the disguise. We have the science of the mind. And we have the power of the universe, which threatens to bludgeon us. If we will not hear the still small voice, we may have to be deafened by the thunder of the splitting or fusing atom. Fission and fusion in the electronic world are a sad substitute for our own failure to master the problems of individualism and relationship. If there is one lesson that the history of the self has to teach us, it is that we cannot rest where we are. At the moment we feel we have found the self, we are already in

[15] Gotthard Booth, "Health from the Standpoint of the Physician," *The Church and Mental Health,* ed. by Paul B. Maves (New York: Charles Scribner's Sons, 1953).

the process of being left behind by the ongoing nature of life.

Man has never grasped this lesson. The result has been tragedy. Will it ever end? Perhaps not. But if ever there were a time when it might, it is our time. Ours could be the thrilling age in which we discover what we have been doing and why, in which we might at last come to know ourselves, the good, the bad, and the different.

3 ✣

The Self in Development

The self in history leads naturally to the history of the self. Our search for the self will now shift its gaze from the history of peoples and ideas to the history of the development of the individual person. It is still a big question whether our search will take us backward toward the past, forward toward the future, or inward to our beings.

This knowledge has arrived through many sources in the last hundred years—the medical and social sciences, the experiences of educators, the insights and observations of adults newly sensitized to the behavior of children. Information is available from experiment, observation, and theory formation, as well as from the personal experiences of patients and of psychiatrists who have first consented to be patients themselves—the psychoanalysts.

Knowledge of man can be classified and presented in numerous ways—in the order of its discovery and formulation, in a developmental scheme of the growth of a person from conception to death, in a cross-sectional scheme that looks at all the interacting forces at a given moment in life. The presentations can be given in terms of a mechanical model, showing the machinelike mechanisms and dynamisms of the human organism and personality. The themes and relationships of a human life or group can also be communicated in terms of history, drama, and myth, using the classic models of ancient writers, poets, and seers. Inevitably, we shall find ourselves slipping back and forth from one style of presentation to the other. In so doing we shall be reflecting the very ambiguity that is man. For man cannot be encompassed by a single diagram. He eludes explanation in any universal sense. He is always *more than* and *other than* the best of our explanations. No matter how far our science and philosophy have led us, there is a sense in which man transcends our fullest formulation of his origin, nature, goal and destiny.

Any reduction of men to a few qualities, therefore, is an oversimplification. But since such a reduction shows us the basic ingredients with which we are working, let us oversimplify by reducing man to four essential qualities. We shall in turn combine these four qualities into "paired opposites," each pair illustrating a tension and a balance in which the human self participates, through which the human self is defined and around which selves enter into transactions with other selves. The dynamic complexity of man will thus be diagrammed and condensed; later we shall examine the meaning of the four poles. But first of all, what are these four qualities we share?

First, *we are individual.* Each of us is a separate and distinct self. Each of us is unique, quantitatively and qualitatively different from each other. None of us can replace another.

Second, *we are interrelated.* Even though we are individual, each of us depends for his existence and identity on that which went before, our ancestors and our parents; further, we depend on our contemporaries to help discover and reveal our own identities.

Third, *we are in equilibrium.* Each of us has a central organizing tendency that pulls together past, present, and future, the inner and outer world, and maintains us in dynamic balance. We are not just parts, but a unified, organic, psychosomatic whole. Our unity is both a source of strength and of weakness. If a part of us is threatened, our whole being is threatened. We get sick with our whole being. We act and think and feel with our whole being, and we sin with our whole being. If one side of us doesn't know what the other is doing, this is not just a sign that the one side is in trouble, but rather that our whole being is in some kind of split condition.

Fourth, *we are in action.* Even though we are in equilibrium, we are also moving in some direction. Physiologically we are somewhere along the path from conception to death. Psychologically, we are moving between infancy and wisdom. Theologically, we are some place between creation and redemption.

These four aspects of the self are paired, and in tension. Individuality is paired and in tension with interrelatedness. Equilibrium is paired and in tension with action. The two pairs of opposites are held together by the self, which they also serve to define. The self, therefore, is to be found at the conjunction of the paired opposites, at the point where contradictions come together.

Where do the contradictions that make up the self begin? On the day of conception, when sperm and egg each cease to be sperm and egg, and join to become something else? On the day when embryologic and fetal development have reached an end point and birth occurs? When the child responds to a smile or recognizes a familiar face? When he knows his own face in a mirror and "mugs" back at himself? When he first walks, talks, fights, rebels? Is it the day of sexual maturity? Of parenthood? Religious conversion? Or death?

Of the contradictions the infant is born with, of the contradictions he meets in his parents, of the contradictions that then grow out of their relationship, two are probably most obviously there from the beginning: the medical terms for them are *symbiosis* and *autism*.

Symbiosis represents the initial merger of mother and child, two beings interdependent in one body.

Autism is a state of extreme separation and isolation into which the child is cast by the cutting of the umbilical cord and out of which he must be wooed into relatedness at a new, psychological level.

When an infant is born, he has just ended a nine-month period of life in which he has done almost nothing for himself. He has not taken a bite of food or drawn a breath of air. He has not walked or crawled one inch through space. From conception until birth the child has been a special kind of parasite upon the body of the mother. His life physically has been fully dependent upon hers. He is so much a part of his mother that her cup of coffee makes his heart as well as hers beat faster. Her activity may make him squirm. Research may disclose that even her pleasures and heartaches affect the disposition of the unborn child.

After birth, the child is physically separated from mother. In contrast with many lower animals, however, he is still almost completely dependent on mother. His linkage continues, but in a new mode. It is no longer a physiological union; it must now be psychological instead. The physical needs must still be met; although the child can breathe, this is about all he can do for himself. He may even have to learn to suck. Every arrangement will have to be made for him by an all-accepting, all-providing environment that consists largely, still, of his mother. Thus there is a sense in which this physical dependence of prenatal life does not fully cease, because mother now takes over in a different way and continues to anticipate the child's needs, feeding his hungers, removing his stresses, and helping him to shift gears from the old prenatal *physical* dependence into the new postnatal state of *psychological* dependence.

Between the physical and psychological linkage is a period through which each of us must pass, when we are no longer part of mother and yet not able to relate to her. We are orphans between two worlds. If we stayed in this state, we would be like the man in Steig's cartoon, curled up in the box, who says, "People are no damn good." To avoid this we must be wooed back into the human race by a mother who affirms to us moment by moment the fact that the world is receptive and ready for our companionship. If the wooing and our response to it are successful, we move forward from the state of newborn isolation into a state of "emotional" dependence—out of which we must be born a second time through a process of individuation. *In other words, there is a double process of being born, first physically and then psychologically, gestating all over again to become a separate self.*

Months will have to pass before the child can in any way separate himself from his psychological dependence. Gradually he will come to control his eating. He will hold up his head, sit up, crawl, stand, and walk. Having heretofore exclusively submitted, he will now begin to refuse as well.

With the first no, whether by word or act, comes the beginning of separation. In the strictest sense, when your child says "no" to you, this is the first time he says "yes" to himself. Independence has begun.

The movement from dependence to independence is more radical in human than in any other form of life. In contrast with many other animals, some of whom are ambulatory and can survive alone at birth, the human newborn is a helpless parasite that would die within a few hours without an available, responsible adult human being, preferably of the female sex. This gross helplessness and enforced dependence leaves its stamp upon us as long as we live. The mark of that stamp is determined by how well mothers care for their children, hearing their cries and "listening with the third ear" for nonverbal indications of need.

Some mothers are more empathic, better able to sense and feel how the child feels inside, than are other mothers. Some mothers—and fathers, too—fear more readily and accurately and answer more quickly and appropriately, some, of course, too quickly and anxiously. Others are, through their own general condition or through their special relations with a particular child, especially inept, obtuse, or negativistic with the child. Still other situations occur in which the child's peculiarities of constitution or a current illness preclude even a superwoman being an effective mother.

It was fashionable a few decades ago to blame mother for everything. Today, we are beginning to take into consideration what mother is given to work with: the mother's own development, her relation with her husband, her child's readiness to let her be a mother and, most of all, the child's "givens" (i.e., that which is given) as an organism.

There are great variations in the "givens" of a child. Is he an easy-crying baby, or does he find it hard to cry? Does he fall asleep readily, or does he need prolonged rocking? Does he stay asleep until he's awakened, or does he return to consciousness with a bang? Some children are more active physically, and more reactive to stimuli. Families vary in their tempo from "molasses-in-January" to "jet-propelled." Scientific experiments have demonstrated that some newborns require ten times as much noise to make them jump as others. Even a child's skin, which is both the boundary and the bridge between the inside and the outside, may be thick or thin, and thus be variably affected by stimuli.

Mothers well know that their babies differ in the amount of protection they need against noise, light, and other possible irritants. Some children go into panic at the color yellow. Others have ecstasy at the feeling of fur. Still others have a complete change in their motor responses in connection with a certain pitch or tempo.

These are only some of the ways in which babies are different from one another even at birth. Some are like hi-fi sets with short-wave and ultra-short-wave and middle-wave reception. Others have only a single narrow band on which they can hear. Most of us, of course, expect our infants to be in the middle range, and we are alarmed if they hear either too much or too little, if they have either an exceedingly thick skin or a too thin one.

In addition to the many variations in *receiving,* there are also many differences in *sending.* Erik Erikson of Stockbridge, Massachusetts, a psychoanalyst, speaks of infants who have a "sending defect," or "low sending power." These babies are not irresistible; in fact, they are easy to ignore. They are just the opposite of babies about whom one says, "I just couldn't take my eyes off that child." Despite adequate vocal cords and noise-making apparatus, they fail to make themselves heard. For a time at least, someone will have to help such a baby by speaking for him or by hearing his unspoken or unvoiced message.

By and large, biological and psychological survival always depends on someone's making up for the immaturity that every infant has at birth. We don't expect the newborn to say, "I need formula and not breast milk." We expect the doctor and the mother together to figure out what the child needs.

It can almost be said that we expect the mother to figure out the problem even more than we expect the doctor to do so. For her observations are intense and intimate ones, but his are limited and governed by what the mother tells him of her own.

Throughout, the doctor's role is a limited one. He examines the child for signs of growth. He determines that limbs and organs are functioning properly. He inoculates the child against future

illness, determines the presence of illness, and treats the child
when he is sick. All of these contributions are important. But
by themselves they are insufficient to produce or sustain life. For
the doctor sees the child infrequently, and though his manner
may be warm and his concern genuine, he sees the child, to some
degree at least, impersonally. To do his job well, the doctor needs
effective clues from the mother—just as the child, in order to live,
needs something from the mother that the doctor cannot give
him. He needs her sustaining love and attention, her watchful
care, her patient limitation, and her stimulation of his total self
to growth and development.

What makes a mother sensitive to the needs of a child? Dr.
Sibylle Escalona, a research psychologist at Albert Einstein
College of Medicine, has called this "reading power," the ability
not only to comprehend the sounds and signs that suggest the
child's needs, but also to read between the lines for the unvoiced,
yet equally vital expressions of need. This ability to understand
the child is one that may be partly innate in the mother, as though
in creating a child, the mother comes to understand the unstated
obligation she has also created, and discovers her inbuilt capacity to meet this obligation. "Reading power" is also acquired
through the culture in which the mother lives. It is there for her
to learn; since childhood she has been exposed to the ready
power of her own mother and others. Furthermore, the culture
demands that she learn it.

Every social group expects certain things of mothers: to raise
healthy, normal, happy children; to protect them from harm until
they can protect themselves; to be tender and loving (although
a few encourage them to be cruel and teasing). Often these expectations of society enhance the mother-child relationship. Sometimes they are a hindrance. Consider, for example, the feeding of
a very new baby. If the mother were to follow her instincts, she
would feed the baby long before its wails threatened to destroy
them both. But at one time, our science-culture decreed that
babies should be fed on schedule—every four hours. Superficially
this seems convenient, especially for the parent. But it is seldom
convenient for the child, who knows more about his need for

food than anyone, and whose digestive needs have not yet come abreast of the parents' clocks and schedules.

Occasionally a mother's appreciation of her child's needs is hindered by some emotional problem. She may resent the child as a rival for her husband's affections. Or she may develop claustrophobic feelings at being closeted with a helpless infant. But sometimes a mother is unable to read the child's needs because she simply doesn't know how.

If a mother is insensitive to her her own bodily sensations, she may have difficulty in imagining how a baby feels. If she cannot permit herself to recognize her true feelings, she will find it difficult to teach her child about his. Many of our feelings—our tastes for food, the textures we enjoy and dislike, the sound level and the temperature of air we find comfortable—are learned. Even our feelings of discomfort are developed by others. A baby crying may only know after being told by his mother that the vague discomfort he had experienced was the sensation which hereafter he will interpret as being "too cold."

Mothers are the persons who interpret us to ourselves. In so doing, they help us become the selves we are.

Most children cannot tell the mothers of these needs to be interpreted to themselves. Parents must learn to read them. To do so, they must be in tune with the child who is uniquely theirs.

"Being in tune" is either automatic or else it is terribly difficult. It calls upon parents of very young children to bear immense burdens—like lighthouse keepers in their long vigils, like radar operators who dare never take their eyes from the screen. Mothers of very young infants are called upon to bind a good many tensions and contradictions. While many of these contradictions grow out of the variations in the child's equipment and reactivity from birth, they also exist in large part as the consequence of the mother's own past. She is herself a being of contradictions. How well she has resolved her own contradictions may determine how well she will be able to accept the child's contradictions and help him to resolve them. However well prepared she is, the contradictions the child presents to her will probably create still more tensions and contradictions in *her*. The emotional state of the mother and the interactions between mother and child are thus of a circular type.

Needs of children do not remain at one level, however; just as a parent begins to think that he has mastered the code for one stage of development, a new one sets in, and the child—or nature—changes the signals. Helplessness gives way to a desire for independence—a demand, raised again and again, that is disastrous to gratify fully or at once. Most parents have judgment enough not to allow a child unlimited freedom when he first demands it. To do so is to terrorize the child, who finds himself without supports, at the mercy of his drives and curiosity.

But to withhold freedom or unnecessarily delay independence is to miss the opportunity of exploiting curiosity to the fullest. Never again can it be fully recaptured.

One of the most zealous mothers I have ever known, the wife of a musician, had a four-year-old son whose cries for help she could not possibly have missed. She was with him all the time. But this devoted mother was simply incapable of recognizing a need that was just as significant to the child as rescue from external peril. That need was for some responsibility of his own.

At four, a child can reach things, dress himself, and make decisions. He desires to express impatience and rage as well as happiness and security. By overindulging and overprotecting this child, by doing everything for him and allowing him to do nothing for himself, this mother had failed to allow her child to grow in one important way. His every wish gratified, he had failed to feel the joy of achievement or the conviction of being what Gerald Pearson, the Philadelphia child psychoanalyst, calls "a going concern." As a result, the child, though given every advantage, is far more immature than most children his age.

A second mother, the wife of a certified public accountant, was extremely sensitive to her son's need to try the unknown. She encouraged self-reliance in every way. As it developed, she encouraged it too much. Whenever the child was sick, she failed to realize that he was, in comparison with his normal state, helpless. She found ways to involve his interest during his convalescence, but she didn't understand his craving for an unusual amount of care and tenderness at this time. As a result, the boy was unable to allow himself the retreat to immaturity and dependence which is a necessary part of the healing process. He could not allow himself to feel or express to his mother just how frightened and hurt and unloved he felt. In one specific instance the mother's inability to read her son's needs hurt even more. The boy's father was injured in an accident while on a business trip, and for several hours they did not know where he was. Today, because the mother failed to perceive her son's fear of losing his father, he has fears he shouldn't have at all. When uncles visit his home, he fears that they are coming to replace his father. When his mother leaves him to go shopping, he fears that she will be injured or that something catastrophic will happen to the house.

Allowing for the optimal regression and progression in the development of a child sounds like an impossible task. It is doubly so if one feels that his own freedom is threatened by the child's claims for same.

Recall, if you will, Jesus' parable of the two sons and their father. The father said, "Son, go work in my vineyard." The first son said, "Father, I go," but went not. The second son said, "Father, I go not," but he went. "Which," asked Jesus, "therefore did the will of his father?" (Matthew 21: 28b-31a. RSV). Both were addressed, both summoned, both commanded. One made the obvious response of obedience without hint of resentment or defiance—and then didn't go. The other responded with a challenge, a retort, a refusal. But his was a gesture of individuality. He said through it, "Father, I do not obey automatically, like a *thing*. I am a person, a separate person. I own myself." Once having established that, he chose to obey.

We're all familiar with the child who says, "I won't" when you tell him to brush his teeth, and then proceeds to brush them surreptitiously, as if to say, "Dad, that's your idea. When I brush my teeth it's going to be my idea." But in this gesture of defiance the child affirms both the father's reality as a person and his reality as a separate self. He says, "You are a person, a person to whom I can say no." And he also says, "I am a person, too, because I can say no, because I have a mind of my own."

For the rest of his life the individual will find himself in the midst of the battlefield between the two warring factions, dependence and independence, which both claim and identify him. Somehow he must resolve, balance, and use the tension between them. When and if he succeeds, he has become a real self, a self that can achieve reconciliation through the binding of contradictions.

All our life we are faced with dramatic examples of the problem of individuality and interrelatedness. All our life we face changes that force us together or apart. These changes are fraught with risk. Sometimes we react with false bravado and compensatory fantasies. I may imagine how strong and powerful I am, that I don't need anyone, that I'm omnipotent. Or my imaginations may develop in the opposite direction and I may dwell upon how evil and wicked and dangerous were the ones on whom I depended and how lucky I am to have escaped their toils.

Sometimes, too, emancipation is only halfheartedly accomplished, as in the story of the little girl who kept walking past a neighbor's front door pushing her baby carriage. The first time around he said hello. The second time around, he said, "Oh, you're back again?" The third time around the man's curiosity was piqued. "What are you doing?" he asked.

"I'm running away," the little girl replied.

"But," said the man, "you just seem to be going around the block, around and around and around."

"Yes, I know," the little girl answered, "I'm not allowed to cross the street."

No matter how halfhearted emancipation may be, it *must* occur; if it does not, the self becomes incomplete, undiscovered, or insane.

What breaks the bond of dependence and thereby enables emancipation to occur? The answer is *action*. Each stage of development demands new balancing of the conflicting forces; as each new point or stage of balance is reached or mastered, there is a new conflict, and the unvoiced but perpetual question of development: "Do I stay here and enjoy the hard-won peace of mind that has been so painfully acquired? Or do I more painfully go on to the new?" "Do I take action?" "Or do I remain 'in irons.' "

The choice is not altogether the individual's. Nature has provided him with at least two forces that are forever pulling and shoving forward—namely, physiological growth and environmental demands. The urgency of forward motion that is built into all living things is what breaks the symbiotic, or dependent bond. You've got to be four now, you can't be three any longer, says the body, and the self must respond.

Maturation and development seem perpetually both at work, maturation depending upon an inbuilt clock or timetable in every body that links us to the human race through our genes, like the cycle of a machine that goes through a sequence one step at a time.

But development occurs in a context; it depends for each new move on the stimuli and responses of our environment. Each stage depends not only on what has gone before but also on what man, and those around him, have made of the circumstances. In other words, each of man's actions demonstrates its meaning in terms of its effect on others, as well as on its source.

Sixty years ago the Western world was shocked by findings of psychoanalytic pioneers that sexuality springs from the earliest days of life. Jeers, snorts, and outraged rejection greeted Sigmund Freud's report of his and his co-workers' observations. Today we find no such argument. We know for sure that sex is integrally linked to all four aspects of the self.

One's sex is part of *individuality,* but a part which one shares with all members of one's own sex. One's sex is a key aspect of all *relationship,* whether it be directly sexual or not.

One's sexuality forms a central focus of one's *equilibrium,* contributing components of identity and energy to the control system of the personality. Finally, one's sexuality constitutes one of the ineluctable inbuilt timetable systems of *action,* driving one on to new stages of development, new loves, aversions, and identifications.

How does this all begin?

Knowing what we already do about the way in which man is in directed action, the way in which he develops out of a long history of his race and his own being, knowing that rarely do even apparently new phenomena lack antecedents and precursors, we should not find it difficult to look back to the first manifestations of sexuality in the child.

We do not, of course, expect to discover full-fledged adult sexuality in the child. On the contrary, we are interested precisely in the kind of sexuality that accompanies each stage of childhood development.

The first aspect of infant sexuality we discover is that of pleasure. We can trace the element of pleasure back as far as the early sucking of the newborn. Within the first few days or weeks of extra-uterine life, the baby begins to show us that he sucks not only functionally, that is to get milk into his body; he also sucks for fun. He shows what seems to be an innate tendency or need to be gratified by lip and tongue and cheek movements beyond those necessary for nutrition.

Non-nutritional sucking needs vary from child to child. Such needs and their probable equivalents have been studied in chickens (non-nutritional pecking) and in puppies (sucking) by Dr. David Levy, an experimentalist in child psychiatry. The studies suggest that while the amount of drive or need to suck may vary from subject to subject, the amount of non-nutritional movement clamoring for gratification will be greater in those cases in which nutrition was not accompanied by gratification. In other words, if the child doesn't get enough pleasure sucking while eating, he'll go after other things—such as his thumb—in between.

By no means all of the pleasure associated with eating is simply the pleasure of sucking. But it is a crucial part, one that lays an essential foundation for sexuality, the capacity to get pleasure from sensitive zones of the body. As the child grows, this pleasure sensitivity moves downward to his anus. He becomes more aware of his bowel movements, getting pleasure from both passing and retaining them, as the tissue of the anus becomes more erogenous. Still later the genitals themselves will take on the primacy of pleasure sensation.

But pleasure from one's own body is not all there is to sex. There is also relationship.

One of the earliest discoveries a child makes is that when he is uncomfortable, someone makes him comfortable. He may be fed, cuddled, cleaned, reassured, spoken to, stimulated, or played with. In any case, he knows it has taken another presence to help him out. We have already talked about this in terms of the mother-child relationship, that "basic psychosomatic unity" as Dr. Therese Benedek, the psychoanalyst, has called it. These early ordinary situations of intimacy are the forerunners of mutual adult intimacy, and especially of the sharing of joys, a crucial part of sexuality.

But sexuality is not limited to bodily pleasure or gratifying relationships. Sexuality is also a matter of identity. It is part of the answer to the eternal question, Who am I? Part of the answer is always "a man" or "a woman" or "a boy" or "a girl." *Identity* with our own sex and *difference* from the opposite sex are two elementary discoveries in our growing self-awareness.

Parents, siblings, and animals are the models by which we classify ourselves and others as males or females, as haves and have-nots with regard to external genitalia. A whole world of mythology grows up in the child's make-believe mind as he tries to account for, justify, and reassure himself about the differences. The need for meaning asserts itself, and explanations that are not forthcoming from others are compensated for from within the self. Frequently the personally conjured explanations are preferred to those which may be more accurate.

As the dominance in the zones of sensitivity shift, so do the preferred modes of gratification or relationship. For example, in the first year, the principal mode is incorporation, literally in terms of food and symbolically in terms of words, sensations, impressions, attitudes, and images. In the second year, expulsion is the predominant mode, be it the expulsion of body contents or of words. The third modal phase is that of intrusion, and this, too, has its literal sexual connotation and its more symbolic social connotation.

It is, however, in the phase of genital (or as the analysts tend to name it) phallic supremacy and of intrusive behavior that interest, sensation, and retention tend to be focused on the sexual parts. For those who do not possess a penis, it becomes an article of envy, often accompanied by resentment of the mother for having given her little girl short change. The child may quickly adapt to her deprivation, saying she prefers to be as she is. For a period she will look down on boys. Whether this is a genuine shift in her orientation toward acceptance, pride, and assurance in her femaleness, or whether it is a defense known as "sour grapes," may make a considerable difference in her later identity as a woman. The boy may be happy to be one of the "haves," particularly if maleness is prized in his family and community. At the same time the very presence of the "have-nots" seems to suggest to him a fear of losing the treasured emblem of maleness.

Not only is childhood sexuality developing around the organ zone and relationship mode, it is also becoming oriented toward an object of the relationship, someone toward whom the love or desire is directed. Initially this object is the self, in its most elementary form, a reflexive infantile organism.

But soon the opportunity occurs to turn this inner-directed love at least partially outward, to a real human person in the real world. This person is the mother or mothering one—the one closest, who feeds, tends, and comforts the child. Later, the father who protects, plays with the child, and is loved by the mothering person comes to be loved by the child.

Both mother and father can be loved by the infant long before their sexual identity and differences are clear to him. When they do become clear, the child tends to favor the parent of the other sex. For the boy this comes naturally. For the girl, this shift means giving up the mother as a loved "object" and taking her as a model for identification. What she can't have she seeks herself to become.

Externally, such early development of the sex and love life proceeds in a fashion largely determined by the mores of the family. But what happens internally when a boy or girl finds his love partner in the parent of opposite sex? The process is thrilling and exciting; it fulfills an innate readiness in both child and parent. But it can also be frightening.

First of all, the child is overawed by the size of the partner. Second, he becomes a rival of the parent of his own sex. Being a rival means resenting and fearing resentment. Resentment entails the combination of wishes to be rid of the irksome rival and the parallel fear of being displaced oneself, But the resented parent cannot be unequivocally hated, because he or she has been loved before. This puts the child in a quandary. He fears both retaliative injury or the loss of love and desertion by the beloved parent of his own sex. Ultimately this quandary compels the child to renounce his first romantic love. He gives way to his bigger rival.

This forced renunciation is termed the resolution of the Oedipus complex. It is made possible by several psychological developments:

First, the selfish, sexual love for the parent of the opposite sex is replaced by a sublimated (desexualized, but pleasant and acceptable) emotion, the same that is felt for members of the parent's sex in childhood and later in adulthood as a marital partner. A boy reasons that while he can't have his mother as a sweetheart, he *can* have her as a mother. Later he can marry a girl like her. Meanwhile, he can enjoy friendship with other females. The axis is thus shifted from sex to friendship, and from present sex to future sex.

Second, the rival of the same sex who is ambivalently loved and hated becomes the model for sexual identification; how the child enjoys vicariously his former rival's access to the renounced partner of the opposite sex. A boy reasons that since he can't have his mother as his wife, he can be like his father who does, and thus participate in the pleasure of the relationship.

Third, a new department of the personality, the superego, develops as the child identifies himself with the parent of the same sex. The superego can be looked upon as a kind of unconscious conscience, a constellation of commands and prohibitions that make their commands just as surely as does an external parent or taskmaster. Its gradual development probably has its first origins with the first experiences of limitation that the child undergoes. Gradually, restraint from without is replaced by controls from within—almost automatic controls.

When the child first obeys in the absence of the parent—when he goes to the toilet by himself or stays on the sidewalk—he shows beginning signs that his superego is developing.

Prior to the resolution of the Oedipus complex, the child's superego is weak, disorganized, and definitely not sex-linked.

Because it holds an inner threat, it becomes strongly organized around one's sexuality as a boy or girl. Now the issue is not just obedience, but one of being manly or womanly, of following a pattern of a loved one whose life is becoming a part of one's own inner life.

We will see how important it is through the next five or six years of life, to puberty and adolescence, for the child to be like those of his own sex. The other sex is condemned with a vengeance. Girls consider boys nasty; boys think girls silly. This is the normal homosexual period of development.

Actually it is a largely desexualized period; the energies previously devoted to sexuality are now available for the growth of the intellect in the crucial early years of school when we are able to learn more rapidly than ever again. The energies are also turned to socialization, with teachers, other adults, and other children, mostly of the same sex. Finally, energies are turned to physical skills, to the sports, games, and tricks that mark us as competitive and co-operative with our own sex.

Puberty, the emergence of adult sexual characteristics, introduces the growing child to a tumultuous phase of adolescence. This in-between period, in which one is neither child nor adult, and at the same time is alternately both, is a time of troubles for most normal children and their families. The body appearance as well as the body image—the picture one has of oneself—is changing. The appearance of one's sexual peers is also changing. Things won't stay still! Parents are too understanding or not understanding enough, too permissive or too controlling, too helpful or too demanding of mature responsibility. Inner sexual urges are controlled by inner prohibitions, outer conventions, and religious taboos. It is at this puzzling time that three tasks confront the adolescent. He must learn to accept his body and its changing function and needs. He must learn to accept adult responsibility. Finally, he must achieve a work function and acquire a vocational identity.

The timing could hardly be worse.

There are many styles that may be followed in the development of the individual. In one sense we are all different; in another we are all alike, possessing common needs, urges, drives: for pleasure, for control, for meaning. If we deny our aggression and pretend we are too good to desire control over others, we lie to ourselves and develop a mask to others. If we deny our pleasure needs and pretend we are not sexual creatures, we deceive ourselves and distort our behavior toward others in turn. If we deny our need for meaning in life and pretend we live only for pleasure or power, we paralyze our minds for thinking in depth and cut ourselves off from critical and creative contact with others in the world of ideas.

In some ways adolescence is like the witchcraft period of history. Energy and enthusiasms are unbounded, but directedness is shaky, fanatical, contradictory, and evanescent. Rather than being integrated, the good and evil of the self are isolated from one another. The Devil is in the flesh, but he is either denied, fought, or gratified. Our culture offers no other recourse. It compels its adolescents to wait for gratification of their yearning; if they don't, the culture teaches them to feel guilty.

Alternations between dependence of an almost infantile type with massive bids for unprepared-for autonomy go hand in hand. The old struggle between individuality and relatedness is almost as intense as the initial struggle between autism and symbiosis in the newborn. Parents are hard put to be stable in the face of such radical teenage vacillation.

Work is as crucial a part of the life of the adult as play is for the child. Aside from its survival and utilitarian elements, it fulfills needed psychic functions of handling energy, of asserting and reinforcing personal identity, of reassuring one of personal worth, of allowing nonharmful expression of aggression toward material things and toward persons with whom one interacts.

Work can be denatured to drudgery or it can be overspiritualized into a sacrament. Realistically it must always have in it two elements: that of play and that of duty. Having them, it fulfills our inner needs both for pleasure and for the feeling of self-approval that comes from conforming to an inner demand or living up to a high ideal.

It is the child's task at this time to begin formulating for himself a type of work that will provide him with elements of both play and duty. His task is not made simpler by our Calvin-

istic puritanical heritage, which makes so many of us dutiful but
joyless about our enterprise.

How the cultural contradictions contribute to personal disunity
is reflected both in man's work identity and in his approaches to
society.

We become suckers for the accepted lie; we are sheep who
follow and never question. We may accede to creeds and conduct,
but we are seldom knowers of the truth or believers in the way
of life.

How we get to be this way grows out of a series of givens
and gifts, out of our biological and social heredity and the way
in which it and our environment have interacted all along.

Some of these interactions are dramatic. Some are mechanical.
Both are necessary, one for ordered stability in our self ap-
praisal and self understanding, the other for imagination and
directedness. If the processes are reciprocal and mutual, then
things may develop smoothly. If they are in marked disharmony,
then we may have trouble. What is most "natural" is of course
the situation in which we're ready for something when the time
comes. In contrast a child may strain to fulfill the myth of an
older brother and fail miserably either because of innate un-
readiness or because the physiological timetable has him sched-
uled for another stop. The mutuality of the two trends, that of
maturation on the one hand and development on the other, the
indispensability of both if anything is to happen at all, makes
us cautious in underrating or overrating either. My genes insure
that I cannot be a lizard. There just isn't a chance in the world,
no matter what my environment. A bad environment insures that
even the best genes will be wasted and fail to manifest or develop
the potential they would have in another milieu. As has been
said, the very finest genes don't do very well in sulfuric acid.

Thus we see that man's nature depends on a "given," his
organism and its environment. But his nature is also dependent
from moment to moment on the people about him and their
"gifts." Living is a function both of the genes that determine man's
potentialities and of his response to the gifts he continues to
receive.

The problems of developing our unique, separate, autistic side will be with us all our lives. Something inside will tug at us when we take our first step, say our first word, first dress ourselves, spend our first night with a friend, first talk back to our parents, first undertake to decide our own destiny. Likewise, the problem of symbiosis, of relatedness, merger, affiliation, will plague us; it will block us from letting ourselves become deeply involved, identified, or concerned with others. It will be so much easier to merge, like the Indian does with God,[1] or simply to withdraw.

To be separate and distinct, related and involved is a lifelong struggle for balance. It is the basis of most major conflicts. Sometimes the conflicts make us go forward. They can also make us sick. The difference is in how we learn and are taught to use them.

---

[1] While merging with God may seem to a Westerner an easy escape from facing the challenges of differentiation into a separate self, the task is not easily accomplished for the Indian.

4 ✳

The Self in Communication

Emperor Frederick, who ruled the Holy Roman Empire during the thirteenth century, was a curious man. Some of the stories of his ranging quests for knowledge are told in Salimbene's *Chronicle*. These experiments are known as "The Follies of the Emperor." One is particularly notable.

Frederick wondered what language had been spoken in the garden of Eden. Had it been Hebrew? Greek? Latin? How was he to find out? The emperor reasoned that since Adam and Eve had been left to their own devices, he need only recreate the circumstances in which they had begun to speak, and he would have his answer. He determined to isolate infants from the moment of their birth, so that they would never hear human speech until they heard their own. To accomplish this, he arranged for several children to be reared by wet nurses; the nurses he instructed to maintain absolute silence.

It is tremendously difficult for a woman to be silent with a child. Nonetheless, the nurses succeeded. According to the account not one of them uttered a single word to any of the children. In other words, the experimental conditions were a success. But the children all died.

What was true for these children is true for all of us. We need others in order to live, and without them we perish. We need them in every level of relationship: in community, in communion, and in pilgrimage. But before we can achieve any needed relationship with others we must be able to communicate with them. Failure in this primary relationship can be catastrophic —and we see this truth demonstrated over and over again in contemporary society, with an unwitting cruelty matching Frederick's.

We know that when children separated from their parents, particularly from their mothers, from the fourth to the eighth months of life, die, the cause of death is not usually conventional disease but lack of relationship. We know from the work of Margaret Ribble, René Spitz, and other child psychiatrists that children reared in foundling hospitals, even under the most hygienic conditions, have a higher mortality rate than other children. They also develop a series of physical, intellectual, and emotional disorders having direct relationship to their age at the time of adoption—to the length of time, in other words, that they have been treated impersonally. We even know that older persons deprived of the most basic form of communication with their world, stimulation, lose their sense of reality and ultimately their sense of themselves.

We don't ordinarily think about the thousands, indeed millions of stimuli we receive each minute—from the tightness of our clothing, the uncomfortableness of our seat, the warmth of a room or the monotonous sound of a voice, yet every one of these serves to confirm that we are here and we are ourselves. Dr. Donald Hebb, a psychologist in Montreal, and Dr. John Lilly, a psychiatrist in Washington, have each managed to isolate volunteers from the real world of objective stimuli by using blinders, earplugs, and other devices. The volunteers developed strange ideas. They heard sounds that weren't there. They saw things that weren't there. They lost their capacity to concentrate, and became seriously muddled in their memory, time sense, and other mental abilities.

Not only must we be assailed moment by moment by a continuing barrage of stimuli; there must also be a certain amount of variety and change of pace in this barrage. The teamster driving his truck along a lonely road at three o'clock in the morning may have plenty of stimuli impinging on his retina, his ear, and the seat of his pants; but because the stimuli are the same ones he has seen and felt and heard since the previous morning, he begins to see red spiders on the windshield.

Our bodies and minds need to be kept awake and alive by

stimuli. Our sanity in a sense depends upon our being continuously and variably spoken to by those around us. *Yet there are forces within us that resist this essential ingredient to our emotional diet.* These forces isolate us from the very contact with people that we need to become and remain ourselves. They are the inner forces constantly with us and in conflict with each other—the pairs of opposites, individuality against relatedness and equilibrium against action. Our troubles begin when any one element of either pair overwhelms its opposite.

Overindividualistic communication is noncommunication: no one else can understand our private language if we have forsaken the human race.

Overrelated communication is barely communication. Unless we are separate selves we have little of value to offer others.

Overequilibrium makes us poor communicators, for we are then so stable that we are not in need of either giving or receiving.

Overdirected action makes us poor communicators, since we may be so goal-focused that we have difficulty finding and relating to others with their own different goals, actions, and directions.[1]

While each of these tendencies, considered by itself, is a problem, all of them, harmonized through communication, are necessary to the discovery of the self. Without such reconciliation, we never learn who we are.

For we are defined by communication, which we may also call reflection. We learn about ourselves by seeing our reflections in others, by noting the feelings we arouse in them, just as we come to know our own features by looking in a mirror.

When a young physician tells me about his work with a patient, I hear not only the answers to my questions about the patient,

---

[1] Professor Outler rightly questions to what extent our present knowledge and methodology enable us to know or evaluate the degree to which a trait or tendency is excessive or deficient. Implicit with all of these alternatives is the assumption of some kind of a golden mean, central norm, or other ideal balance. As a matter of fact, we need to think through the meaning of such an ideal of balance and its implications for individuality as well as to develop empirically both the methods for study and data from studies about precisely what are the relative strengths of the tendencies in question.

but also some answers to my unvoiced questions about the kind
of doctor he is. If he overreacts to a patient's anxiety, he suggests that he is anxious himself. If he underreacts to a patient's
hostility, he may be revealing a fear of disclosing his own.
Similarly, when a mother talks to me about her child, she is
telling me about herself as well as the child. If she complains
that he can never let her out of his sight, she may be reflecting
her own inability to leave him alone. If she ignores his excessive messiness, she may be reflecting her own unsatisfied need
for this very form of gratification.

Communication requires two givens. One is a body that is
physiologically ready to receive and send messages. The other
is an environment in which there will be a response to these
messages. It is pretty hard to keep on sending messages from
a radio tower day after day if one doesn't have a conviction
that someone, somewhere is listening. It is equally hard to keep
listening to the radio if one doesn't have the conviction that
someone, somewhere is going to be sending. The same is true
for the self in communication. For selfhood to occur and be
maintained, a person must be continuing in communication, and
the environment must be continuing to accept him as communi-
cator.

According to the Bible, God creates the reality of us as he
calls us by name. According to scientific information about human development, the child learns who he is by being addressed;
he learns who the other is by addressing him and evoking response. Thus communication comes to us on many levels—on
the organic, the psychological, the social, and the spiritual. God's
word, mother's word; God's voice, mother's voice; my voice,
your voice—all speak and "hear" us into life.

But communication need not always be in the form of the
direct, spoken word. It can also be indirect. Indeed, the many
forms of indirect communication are often more effective than
direct communication in getting across deep feelings in crucial
moments.

Mary Tully, associate professor of religious education at
Union Theological Seminary in New York City tells the story
of the little boy who went to lunch with his mother and sister

in a restaurant. After the sister and the mother had given their orders, the waitress turned to the boy and asked, "Young man, what will you have?" But before he could reply his sister said. "I'll order for him." The waitress repeated her question to the boy. But again his reply was stifled, this time by his mother, who said, "I'll order for him."

The waitress, undaunted, repeated her question to the boy. "Young man," she said firmly, "what will you have?"

"A hamburger," the boy said.

"And how would you like it? Rare, medium, or well done?"

"Well done."

"And what would you like on it—mustard, pickles, onions, relish, or catsup?"

"Mustard, pickles, onions, relish, catsup—the whole works!"

The waitress repeated the order, "One hamburger, well done, coming up—with mustard, pickles, relish, onions, catsup—the whole works!" And then she walked off to fill the orders.

The boy turned and exclaimed in astonishment to his mother, "Gee, mommy, she thinks I'm real!"

The waitress had communicated respect, sensitivity, and acceptance, without using one of these words.

Communication may be even more indirect, even less verbally explicit. We are all aware of the reassurance that sometimes comes from the mere presence of another person. We have all experienced the signals of danger that are imparted by gesture or involuntary physical movement. Indeed, there are hundreds of ways in which we get across to another person whether we are listening, hearing, or caring, all without the use of explicit words. There is, for example, the story of the man who wanted to start a jade collection. He was a very rich man, but he didn't want to be cheated, so he determined to seek instruction in jade grading from the most famous jade connoisseur in the world. Through a friend he was introduced to an expert on jade, and learned that the course consisted of twelve lessons and would cost a thousand dollars. "That's all right," he said. "How do the lessons go?"

"You come here every week for one hour, and in twelve weeks you will know how to evaluate jade," his teacher responded.

Each week the man went for his lesson, and each week his

teacher placed a different piece of jade in his hand and walked from the room. That was all. At the end of the eleventh session, the student was so angry he complained bitterly to the friend who had arranged the lessons. "You led me astray. You let me think this man was really an expert, and look what I've got for my pains—eleven hours of holding a stupid piece of jade in my hand."

Together they went for the twelfth lesson. Again the jade expert simply put a piece of jade in the hands of his pupil, and walked out of the room.

"You see?" said the pupil to his friend. "Not only has he wasted my time and money for the first eleven hours, but to add insult to injury, in the last hour he gives me a fake piece of jade." Communication had occurred.

Another example of nonverbal communication is that of the mother who places a spoonful of food within the half-opened mouth of the infant, and automatically and unwittingly opens her own mouth in the process. The mother's communication is by identification with the child who, at the same moment, is beginning to experience identification with her. The same thing is happening to each of us and continues to happen to us—perhaps every day, perhaps more often than we will ever know. As the late George Herbert Mead, who was professor of social philosophy at the University of Chicago pointed out, communication becomes both significant and meaningful when it succeeds in arousing in the person to whom the communication is being sent, or within the pair who are communicating, common feelings, common experiences, common actions that are recognized both as common and as being confirmed within the being of the other. Here is evidence that when I address you, I address myself. And when you listen to me, you are listening to yourself. In other words, when I speak to you I feel that I am heard and I feel that my speech becomes meaningful to you *if and when within you are elicited some of the actions that are contemporaneously being elicited within me.*

This state of communicating is sometimes called *resonance* or *empathy.* It is likened to a set of unstopped piano strings, which will selectively reverberate or respond to a tone that is the same as that for which any one of these strings is set. In other words, one can sing to the piano, and it will sing back to him. In human dialogue one elicits in the person the response at the very moment that the communication has gone across. Reverberation is the necessary ingredient for all communication. It is especially indispensable for nonverbal communication—which, in turn, is indispensable in the rearing of children, the creation of a therapeutic milieu for very sick people, and the achievement of an effective relationship between a patient and his psychotherapist.

Despite the importance of a patient's verbalizations in the recovery process, there are times when the verbal seems to block or replace real communication. Despite the necessity of speech in the development of the personality from infancy onward, there are elements of the nonverbal which seem to undergird and transcend the verbal, and are essential for healthy development. For example, it is little reassurance to a child who is really suffering to be told that "it doesn't hurt." If, however, a child's relation to his mother is such that her words and voice transmit to him a sense of security and love, then perhaps even real physical pain is allayed.

For a number of years I have made a particular study of a group of schizophrenic children. These children are characterized by an early or innate disturbance in their capacity to relate, communicate, play, and learn. They may be nontalkers or delayed talkers; they may talk for a time and then cease to speak, or they may talk precociously and almost constantly. In this last variety, speech is not used for social communication in any ordinary sense but is usually made up of long speeches memorized in the past and anachronistically regurgitated out of context. This phenomenon, which is called "delayed echolalia," is only one of the autistic symptoms seen in such children.

The concept of early infantile autism implies that the child lives to himself. He may be accurate in his memory, dexterous in his movements, and graceful in his gait, but he is without appropriate feelings for others. It is sometimes said of these children that they have invested their own psyche with the energy that others invest in relationship with persons outside of themselves.

While the autistically schizophrenic child may be withdrawn, negativistic, repetitive, resistant to change, or noncommunicative, there are other manifestations of schizophrenic disorder in children.

Almost the polar opposite of the autistic child is the one known as the *parasitically symbiotic*. This child displays a pathological prolongation, intensification, and distortion of the normal mother-child symbiosis (which we described in Chapter II). This relationship is necessary for survival in the human species during the first six to twelve months of life. Then it should atrophy to permit the orderly development of independence. But for the symbiotic child, mother remains a part of his ego as late as the eighth year. His normal emancipation and development of separate identity never takes place.

The autistic child never becomes a part of his world. The symbiotic child never leaves the oceanic oneness with the matrix of origin. He refuses to become a separate self.

In these children, as in many adult schizophrenics, words do not initiate cure. Neither their own words—which may never be verbalized, or at least never verbalized communicatively—nor those of the therapist seem to say very much at first. What helps more than words, my colleagues and I have found in our treatment of some forty schizophrenic childen in recent years, are such nonverbal communicators as acceptance, limitation, and spontaneity.

By *acceptance* I mean simply that the therapist saw both bitter and sweet in the child—and let the child know that he saw both.

By *limitation* I mean that the therapist was not fully permissive. He did not permit his patient's or other children's comfort and safety or, for that matter, his own to be impaired. He called undesirable behavior to the attention of the child, applied appropriate control techniques, and stopped the child from going too far.

By *spontaneity* I mean that the therapist acted naturally, in the context of the moment and out of the available fullness of his own resources, including mirth, tenderness, stimulation, or anger.

For communication to occur something more than words is called for. The most meaningful and indispensable contents of communication are preverbally acquired. All too often words become separated from the feelings to which they ought to refer. In fact we rarely express concern about the most basic events until long after we have forgotten their reality. How many recall the taste of mother's milk, the feel of a wet diaper, or the intra-uterine enveloping by fluid? Bits may be recovered in a dream or fantasy, but by and large memories are lost. Indeed, it may well be in parenthood that one first rediscovers that he knows how a baby feels, but cannot tell how he knows— probably through having been a baby himself and having the feelings recalled by the new member of the family.

Communication without words has been reported countless times in religious experience. To what extent this is a spontaneous, uncontrolled phenomenon, no one can be sure. I believe, however, that there is relationship if not identity between nonverbal communication and common grace, a quality or power that theology sees as coming to man from God.

We have seen that communication can be not only direct but often indirect; not only verbal, but also nonverbal—through accidental or deliberate gestures and signals, through empathy, resonance, and the presence of a significant person. Going one step further, we should also recognize that communication, which is most often external, can occur *within ourselves*.

One may have dialogue alone. We have all had the experience of lying awake in bed, planning the next day's activity. We have all consoled ourselves by pleasant memories at times in which we have felt cut off and abandoned. In such situations one has dialogue with the memory of previous dialogues, with an absent other, a person or being who is loved or hated. One can evoke the reassuring relationships of the past, or the confident expectations of the future that we call trust.

A great many dialogues are carried on with the self as fantasy. This kind of dialogue can be either dangerous or creative. It is dangerous when it is entirely separated from reality, when it so preoccupies one that it inhibits action. It is dangerous when it is not under some degree of voluntary influence or when it runs off in all directions. Then it becomes frightening to us, signalling our disequilibrium or disease. But inner dialogue is useful whenever it has relevance to the real world and is not re-placing reality.

Indeed, the ability to maintain inner dialogue may well deter-mine survival in those extreme situations in life that so infre-quently occasion massive self-discovery. Each of us must feel shame for the mankind that has produced a concentration camp into which even one human being can be thrown. Yet out of these terrible life stresses sometimes emerge insights into the nature of life for which all we can do is gratefully thank the prisoner returned from the dead. Both Bruno Bettelheim, a child psychologist of Chicago, and Viktor Frankl, the Viennese founder of the logotherapy school of psychotherapy, were imprisoned by the Nazis during World War II. To survive the indignities heaped upon him, Bettelheim steeled himself to observe them as clinically as he would a scientific experiment. Observation and under-standing became for him a means of survival. Frankl pre-occupied himself with an internal scrutiny of his past values and with recollections of his beloved wife, whose fate he did not know. Many prisoners perished in the concentration camps, many lost both their minds and their faith. But Bettelheim and Frankl found a means of transcending their circumstances.

Inner dialogue may occur at moments of self-examination, of spiritual ecstasy, or of intellectual illumination. The process is essential to the working through of any problem. But whatever its setting, internal dialogue is never really carried on alone. For it takes as references all that has gone before in the life of the individual engaged in self-communication. And his ex-periences are inseparable from the world and its people who surround him.

There is a great lesson here for all communication. It becomes meaningful and effective only when carried on between people who truly care what they hear from and say to others.

Not all communication should or can be at such depth. To be at this level all the time would be wasteful, impossible, and unendurable. It would be fantastically inefficient. For example, when I dial the telephone to find what time it is, I'm interested only in the numbers that are going to come back to me over the phone. I'm not really interested in the woman or tape recorder that utters them. This is communication in which the other is an object, not a subject. Communication is often *about* things, but real communication is always *between* persons.

Herein is the key to communicating, the first step in the discovery and completion of the self: *Hearing the other as subject means hearing him as a person.*

Too often, however, we find that persons communicating with other persons regard them as things. If it is true, as we have said, that we are defined by others, then here is where many persons get lost in the search for themselves. In failing to communicate with others, they fail to complete themselves.

To readers familiar with the works of the great Jewish theologian, Martin Buber, this theme will not be unfamiliar. To those not acquainted with Buber, his importance can quickly be established through an opinion of many Protestant clergymen that he has had more influence on Christianity than any Jew since Paul. Buber wrote a book many years ago called *I and Thou*.[2] J. H. Oldham,[3] the foremost spokesman for Protestant unification, has said of it: "I question whether any book has been published in the present century the message of which, if it were understood, would have such far-reaching consequences for the life of our time."

What Buber did in *I and Thou* was to establish the theological validity of a psychological principle. Buber contended that self-concern does not provide self-fulfillment. We become real, full selves only when we relate to others, he declared, for it is only through the reaction of others that our own existence is confirmed. Again, it is like seeing one's own image in a mirror; to be fully real we must see our reflection in others. Thus, we are interdependent in the quest of the self. *We* cannot really be unless our being is affirmed by others, and they will not affirm us in a manner that makes us sure of our own existence *unless we affirm them in a manner that totally acknowledges them for*

[2] Edinburgh: T. & T. Clark, 1937; 2nd ed. New York: Charles Scribner's Sons, 1958. Cf. also Buber, *Between Man and Man* (Boston: Beacon Press, 1955).

[3] J. H. Oldham, *Real Life Is Meeting* (London, The Sheldon Press, 1942), p. 28.

themselves. If we *use* them, they are like doormen or ushers. But if we accept them as they are, then we achieve a confirming relationship that is acknowledged by the familiar address "thou."

To achieve such depth requires uninhibited ability to communicate.

Token communication has a definite maintenance value; it is an absolute necessity in order to get downtown and back. We must have communication that is automatic, stereotyped, repetitive. We get out of someone's way and we expect him to get out of our way. Such automatic gestures are requisite to survival. If suddenly these techniques should drop out of sight, and if we should expect to have intimate conversation on a person-to-person level with people all the way downtown, we'd never get there.

On the other hand, these same maintenance communications can be carried on *as if* we really knew and respected the other person, *as if* we cared for him personally. There is a difference between token communication of a cold type and token communication of a warm type, and this difference is sometimes expressed in the word *courtesy.* A certain *graciousness* can permeate even automatic gestures, a certain *warmth* can help us to treat the other person as if we knew him well enough for him to be personally meaningful to us. The terrible discourtesy of thing or token relationships minus the element of this grace is what frightens so many people when they come to large cities or visit towns in which their way of speaking is unfamiliar.

But even the consolation of courtesy wears thin so long as communication remains on the "thing" level. At some point every individual must achieve a relationship with a person as person. I recall a young woman who worked as a food handler in a cafeteria where a number of my associates and I once ate. There are no pickles sour enough to make a person's face look as grim as hers. Every individual anticipating his meal would be confronted with this chilling visage, and doubtless gastric juices ran cold. We decided to thaw her out. Every time we received our food, we did so with warm and full graciousness. "My, that looks good," we'd say. Or, "My, what a crowd you've had today." And later on, "You must be tired." Or, "How was your vacation?" We really worked at it. After about a year we were convinced we were really getting somewhere, because every once in a while she would smile, just a little fleeting smile, and then apologetically cover it up with a scowl. Two years later she was "all fixed." And then we learned. She'd been in psychotherapy the whole time.

Now nobody knows how much our little effort was responsible for the success of her therapy. But it must have helped. At some point the token relationships became genuine, and they became genuine because we cared. What started out as an experiment became a relationship of concern. She no longer was our guinea pig; she was somebody we liked, and we liked her because we had communicated with her. We all came to know each other as persons.

We cannot live in a world that is made up of the dramatic picture-language of feelings alone. We need a world that is concrete, accurate, and dependable. We cannot constantly maintain the tension of intimacy and dramatic identification. A great many of our relations to persons may and must occur in the objective mode. We will, no matter what we do, think of some people as "things." However, the basic, indispensable and ultimate in relationships are those between two persons who see one another as real in their own right, who have the capacity to feel the other's feelings, see through the other's eyes, and hear through the other's ears.

Such intimacy is too much for any of us to endure as a steady diet. But all of us must have some of it, or die.

5 ❈

The Self in Community

We have looked at the self in irons, at how man, complex and loaded with conflicts, is all too often locked into a self-made prison. We have spoken of the self in history, of how man viewed his neighbor, his God, and himself across time. We have talked of the self in development, of some of the ways in which each of us personally comes to be. And we have looked at the self in communication, at how each of us learns to hear and speak to others.

But communication with a single "other" is not enough. Communication draws its fuller meaning when we speak and are spoken to by the community that we call our own. Community implies a certain commonness, similarity, sharedness, participation, belonging, and corporateness—all of which make it possible for us to become, survive, and thrive as selves. An old Jewish saying, "Ein Mensch ist kein Mensch (One man is no man)," is as true today as when it was first uttered.

Community involves the individual even before his birth. In addition to providing protection for his mother during pregnancy and childbirth, the community approves of her as a vessel for its own perpetuation. The newborn is greeted not only by his own parent, but by the larger family of siblings, ancestors, neighborhood, culture and tradition—all of which are made and perpetuated by, and make and perpetuate, the community.

In Christian baptism or christening, as in parallel rites of naming which occur in most if not all cultures, the new arrival is recognized as a creature of promise (or threat) and receives provisional acceptance. He or she is accepted on faith as a future participant in the group—usually on the basis of the group's trust and expectations of the parents' desire and ability to rear the child to be a good Missourian or Zulu or Presbyterian. The child can say or do little about being cast into the special community of his parents and their people. He depends upon them to justify this fate through their reception of him and interpretation to him of the world into which he is received.

From his parents he first learns of the protective (or non-protective) character of his community, its culture, folkways, traditions, language, history, ideology, rites, and worship. This is an unasked-for indoctrination, but an inevitable one. And try as a family may try to conceal, modify, or deny its community in interpreting life to its child, a child will inevitably discover the community or the substitute for it which the family wittingly or unwittingly provides.

But the community of family and social inheritance has accepted the newborn (who soon becomes a child and an adolescent) only provisionally. He is in and of the community but not fully identified with it until he "comes of age"; until he is initiated into the community's society he is still living on his parents' promises to the community and the community's promises to him. One day he must choose and be chosen, commit himself and receive commitment from the community that is his and whose he is.

These mutual choices and commitments of the young person and his community (called variously initiation, *rites du passage,* and confirmation) have gone on for centuries. They are the processes by which the person's identity is given and received, by which he confirms and is confirmed as *who* and *what* he is. In this process he can say, "Yes, I am one of thee," and the group in answer says responsively, "Yes, verily, thou art one of us and are called by our name, and our God and people are your God and your people."

But community, to be full community, is not simply a matter of birth and identity confirming. It is also a matter of *healing.*

The early Christian community experienced and communicated a special kind of healing—special because it was complete: physical, moral, spiritual, and psychological. In Christian community the individual is seen as a whole being. The community suffers together with him whether he suffers in an aspect we call mind, or an aspect we call body, or an aspect we call spirit. Whatever their genesis, the wounds of the individual are those of the community, and healing that is a forgiving kind, an accepting-in-spite-of, goes on.

The message of the Early Church was not that man could be so awfully good, but that he could be so loved in spite of his failure to be good, and that the more he could allow himself to be loved, the more his possibilities for good could be enhanced.

"The good news" that the fellowship of Christians (called the *Koinonia*) preached to their flock was that God was with them, that he had been all along despite man's attempt to deny his dependence on God, to *distance himself,* or to erect religious barriers between himself and his God. And this news was dramatized by God's coming in Christ, and Christ's fellowship with men as they were; the love that was stronger than hate or fear or guilt; the openness that was more powerful than man's need to encapsulate himself, the welcome to the outcast, the slave, and the pagan. These all bespoke a new dimension in community, one that was supposed to break down barriers and admit the stranger even while it transformed him and was itself transformed in the process.

How well the Early Church succeeded in erecting this kind of Koinonia is recorded in the pages of the New Testament and the writings of the Early Fathers. How quickly and easily it failed in certain aspects is a reminder again and again of man's tendency to spurn both the givens and the gifts of the good life that God has offered.

Able to raise women to a new estate of equality, to accept slaves as spiritual equals, to speak to Samaritans and pagans, to love enemies and strangers, the Christians were still intolerant of heretics and even mild deviants. Zealous to preserve the truth, they lost again and again the unity and the concord that was the injunction of both the Lord who prayed that the flock might be one even as he was one with the Father, and of the Apostles Paul and John, who saw the Church as one Body whose members' sonship was seen in their love of one another.

Yet somehow the Church moved in the right direction. Despite a tendency toward perfectionism that sometimes forgot what man was, the Church could usually take into account human nature in a realistic way. Despite the periodic attempts to discredit and philosophize away the body, to negate the intensity of man's negative feelings and encourage him to conceal them, there was recurrent realism and honesty. St. Paul expressed it in his awareness of the internal warfare, the contradictory principles within man. Where sin abounded, said St. Paul, "grace did much more abound."

Out of honest recognition of the contradictions came great power for life, great new surprises. The presence in the Church of a knowledge of the depth of evil, of anger, of lust, of pride, made it possible to accept man as given, in spite of the unacceptable in him.

This openness to surprise is one of the most characteristic marks of a truly healing community. The moment we stereotype a healing process we stop it, or at least interfere with its fullest expresson. If the ministry and the Church become so preoccupied with discipline and theory that they become obscurantist, moralistic, or mechanical, the caring is lost; if they become preoccupied with the caring at the expense of discipline, they become ecstatic, sentimental, or lawless.

But amidst this tension between discipline and caring, which make for disciplined caring, is the element of surprise. For Christians, this is very often seen as Grace.

The very thing that makes us human is this capacity for the unexpected. What shows that we have slipped a little in our humanness is when we are bowled over by the unexpected, or when we no longer startle ourselves by what we say.

Openness to surprise is one way of talking about flexibility in a community. It means that the community is not static, not fixed, not unchangeable, not "as it was in the beginning, is now, and ever shall be, world without end." If a community is fixed and final and unchanging, it is not a living community. It is an archaic cross section viewed at a point of time as if for all time.

How, then, can we achieve the mean? How can we live at the interfaces between the constant and dependable, which we must have as a baseline for life, and the surprising, the flexible, the adaptive, and the emerging, which we need to make life live? I would like to suggest that we can do it through dramatic acts of participation and identification with the community, whether these are acts of drama, reading, reciting, or taking bread together. These are the acts by which we symbolize and concretize what our theology teaches abstractly and our everyday life deals with existentially. They are meetings in which we bring together the pieces and particles and make them one, where we relate the general to the very particular, to the concrete here-and-now. We call these acts of meeting "worship."

A famous Roman Catholic lay theologian, Hilaire Belloc, has likened the mass (and I would liken all of worship) to play. It is in play that an individual is forever making it possible for himself to live at the interfaces between fantasy and reality, between past and present, between self and other, because in play one can try a role for fun and not for keeps. He can reverse or turn the tables, not only on the other but on himself, can engage in "reality testing" without enduring the burden of reality itself. He can find out what it is like to be on the inside *from* the inside and yet never commit himself unless he wishes. So in worship the whole community can be itself, and yet act in a kind of corporate play at the same time—and in the process speak beyond itself to a larger concept.

Often we forget this larger concept, as in the story of a father praying in a house of worship beside his son. The little boy is praying softly, the father loudly. The father nudges him and says, "Talk louder." The little boy replies, "I'm not talking to you."

In worship we are not talking *just* to each other. We are talking through each other to God. To put it as Martin Buber does, the shortest line to God is the longest line we can draw around our neighbor. To put it as Jesus did, "How can a man love God whom he has not seen if he does not love his brother whom he has seen?"

It is not enough just to love; we must also be able to recognize the difference between loving and pretending to love, between true nonhostility and covered-up hostility.

In our community there is a form of kindness to others that

we think of as an act of love, but that is frequently a crucial act of hate. It occurs when, out of an exaggerated sense of noninvolvement, we let another person come to a slow boil; and then wonder with raised eyebrows why he is so upset. In other words we "eliminate" his hostilities by avoiding them. The hostilities, of course, do not go away. They persist, they grow, until ultimately we must deal with them in a far more intensified version.

The method by which communities handle hostility vary greatly. In some, a high value is placed on its use in competition, in war, in hunting, and in work. In others, hostility is concealed, denied, and turned indirectly on the self or various scapegoats. Few communities seem to be altogether devoid of hostility; few are able to put it to good use. One that does come close is the Senoi tribe, an isolated Malayan people described by Kilton Stewart, anthropologist and psychologist. The Senoi illustrate two important dimensions of community, those of *openness* and of *meaning*. They have managed through a number of methods, circumstances, or accidents, to remain relatively unaffected by the turmoil of the world. In their valleys and mountain fastnesses they have escaped involvement in major conflict; their people do not seem to need to war upon each other. They have a very low degree of crime by their own definitions of crime, and an equally low incidence of mental illness. Perhaps by our definitions and standards their entire culture would be seen as mentally ill. On the other hand, in contrast with America where the majority of all hospital beds are used for the care of the mentally ill, the Senoi are not troubled with emotional and mental deviation as a community problem.[1]

The Senoi family is exceedingly close. Father and mother both take a keen interest not only in what the child does but also in what he thinks, fantasies, and dreams. The Senoi believe above all in the mastery of reality through coming to terms with the dream.

A Senoi child may tell his parent one morning, "I don't have any bananas today because Johnny stole them in my dream." And Daddy might suggest, "Well, you go and tell Johnny that you didn't like that, and that he'd better make it right today, or at best in tonight's dream." And so the boy would go complain to

[1] Kilton Stewart, "Dream Theory in Malaya," *Complex*, 1951, pp. 3-15.

Johnny, who would accept the dream as part of the real world. "I didn't realize this had happened," he might say, "but if it happened, I'll make it right." They may fight, of course, but the dream in any event is taken seriously. The dream is a community party line to which everyone is connected and responds.

While such a dream schemes denies an individual privacy, at the same time it creates the possibility for making peace before war begins. By American standards the community becomes a little bit crazy by confusing fantasy with reality; yet there is another sense in which the community has no problem any longer about the difference.

A Senoi culture will work as long as the dreams of each member of the culture are acceptable to the others or can be interacted upon. When a foreign note or foreign body is intruded, either from outside or from some kind of spontaneous emergence from within, this can make trouble. Even then the dream process works on it.

The Senoi does more than use the dream individually and socially. He links together the individual and the social use. For example, a child is directed to dream, he is directed to accept his dream, his dream evolves and he engages in dream thinking. Stewart likens this to the biblical "as a man thinketh in his heart, so is he."[2]

Not only do the Senoi people handle their interpersonal problems through the mastery of the dream, they also deal with sociological issues such as that of the contact of alien cultures. While in such instances there is usually intense conflict and anxiety for both of the cultures involved in the encounter, the Senoi people have a means of overcoming this difficulty through the dream.

An example grows out of what happened when a Senoi group was faced with the contact of the Muslim Malayans and the issue arose as to whether they were to wear the sarong and to prohibit the eating of pork. The head shaman had a dream in which a peaceful solution to the conflict emerged. It was a healing dream and it suggested a healing dance—the Chim Chim dance. Dramatization through dance was relaxing physically and

[2] Personal Communication.

socially. In this dramatization were elucidated the problems and their solutions. The dance reduced the differences between the two cultures and provided for an outcome which rivaled that of the highest solutions of individual psychology and modern sociology. It also prevented anxiety, guilt, schism, and perhaps even bloodshed.

The solution did not come by accident. It emerged out of the background of centuries of trusting the dream and directing the dream. This illustration indicates how the Senoi both directs his dreams, trusts his dreams, and shares his dreams. He uses them to share his life's problems in a way that approaches the highest type of social thinking that the world has evolved.

No young Senoi is initiated into the group until he is able not only to control his own dream characters, but also able to receive from them. His dream characters must give him a song with words and music, a dance and a design which he draws on a piece of wood. These must have both an original character and a high standard, and he continues to try to dream and receive from his dream characters, until the dream characters are not only under his control, but also have given him a socially acceptable contribution.

Stewart sees the Senoi culture as approaching the Christian church directly, "in their basic concept that if a man will tell his dreams, will co-operate with his fellows when he can, and when he cannot, oppose them with good will, he will be able to conquer all the forces in the spirit world." Stewart likens this to Jesus' teaching that "the kingdom of heaven is within you." Christian doctrine teaches that when we have in us the mind of Christ, we have overcome the forces of evil, "the principalities and powers" —"the spiritual rulers in high places." Hence, Christians become "more than conquerors."[3]

Dramatic and dream communication are not always successful and they depend for their success upon a sharing culture or at least a mutual openness to sharing on the part of both sides.

There is the story of the trapper welcomed by an Indian tribe at the banks of the Mississippi. As they smoked together, the trap-

[3] Personal Communication.

per dreamed off into a haze and was put to bed. In the morning the Indian chief asked him, "What did you dream?"

"I dreamed you gave me the peace pipe."

"Well, White Brother, we have a custom in our tribe that whatever you dream, you shall have; so if you dreamed it, you shall have it."

The next night they again smoked the pipe of peace, and the following morning, the Indian said, "White Brother, I had a dream last night. I dreamed you gave me your gun."

The White Brother scratched his head and decided it was the better part of valor to say, "All right, if you dreamed it, Red Brother, you shall have it."

And so it went. The next morning the white man got the squaw. The morning after that the Indian got the liquor. Finally, one morning, the white man said, "Red Brother, I dreamed last night that all the land from this river, as far as one can go to the great blue waters, you gave to me."

The Indian scratched his head and said, "White Brother, if you dreamed it, you shall have it, but I'm not going to dream with you any more."

But against the possibility of such troubles caused by the intrusion of foreign bodies is the virtue that the earliest inklings of community trouble are bared at once. Each little concern is dealt with as it arises.

Another unusual type of mystic community is Hasidism, an eighteenth-century central European movement. The word Hasidism, meaning "pious ones," actually goes back to the first century B.C. as a tradition within Judaism. The tradition more or less died out from the time of Christ until it reappeared among the Jewish people of the ghettos of middle Europe.

Three separate forces had ripened the Jews for new intellectual ferment. One was a recent and painful history of false alarms regarding the coming of the Messiah. A second was the external force of the Enlightenment itself, from whose scientific and intellectual discoveries came demands that faith be informed by reason, and that tradition be overthrown in favor of new light from the non-Jewish area. Finally, there was a kind of cabalistic—quasi-magic, quasi-religious—influence upon the Jewish community that sought to convince Jews that they could arrive at some special knowledge of how to influence the world in their favor.

In the midst of this ferment, about 1720, there came to prominence a young and relatively nonintellectual rabbi, the Baal Shem Tov, the Master of the Good Name. The very thing that at first terrified people about him ultimately drew them to him. He was alive. He did not believe in tradition, unless it was a living tradition. He disregarded his own lessons in order to play with children and take them to and from school. His personality set the community on fire, and a group formed around him, its members developing ultimately into the spiritual leaders, educators, adjudicators and cultural leaders of the community. These leaders dared to propound, and their communities to demonstrate, that instead of the afterlife, they should hallow the commonplace, the here and now.

It was a community of spontaneity in which there was a great deal of singing and dancing and even drinking together. Religious services were hilarious and, at times, ecstatic. It was a community in which not only did man feel under God's law and indeed under His demand and judgment; it was also a community which felt God should and could be called to account, and in which the rabbi felt quite comfortable in talking back to God in the name of his congregation—asserting the claim on God that the community made.

It was a community in which gradual decay proved its undoing; gradually the Zaddikim ceased to be saint-rabbis and became magic-rabbis and obscurantists. But even in the present-day remains of the Hasidic type of faith, there is a remnant and a relic of something of the joy and the spontaneity that these people had together, so that they could laugh in their faith and revel in their stories, which we know as the Hasidic tales.

One of these will give a sense of the community they characterized, uniting the fragmented into the larger whole, making the lonely feel he belonged to a center that was unshakable. Before the Baal Shem died, he commissioned one of his rabbis to wander for an indefinite period of time in search of truth. He was to be without regular income and dependent on each day's gifts. The rabbi protested to no avail. Off he went finally, wandering from town to town until he came to the outskirts of a city in which he had heard there was a very wealthy Jew. In this city the Jews were in a distinct minority, but the rich Jew was respected by Jews and non-Jews alike. Many times he gave large dinners to which the whole Jewish population came eagerly because the host always had an interesting visitor who spoke.

When the wandering rabbi arrived at the rich man's house, he was made very comfortable. "We'll have a big party tonight," the rich man said. "You will be the guest of honor. You'll tell us some story about the Baal Shem."

The prominent man promised the rabbi all kinds of gifts and presents for his speech. But when the time came to speak the rabbi could not open his mouth. The guests were cynical but the host, however, said, "Friend, I understand that it's hard to talk tonight. Try tomorrow."

So he tried the next day. And again he could not speak a word. The third night came and went, and he could not speak. And so, sadly he left. But even though he had not told a single story, his host provided him with a beautiful carriage and let him be driven away to the next city. Just a few hundred yards outside the gates he suddenly came alive. He returned to the host and said, "I can tell you what has happened."

So the rabbi began. "When the Baal Shem was alive, once in the middle of the night we took a very hurried journey. We came to a city and rapped on a door. It was just before daybreak and we would not be admitted. A woman said the Jews were being persecuted and they dared not let us in. We forced our way in, and found that the people of the house had hidden themselves everywhere. On this particular day there was to be a public celebration and a sermon by the Cardinal, in the Square which the house faced. It had been said that any Jew found on the street would be killed.

As daybreak came we opened and looked out through the cracks in the barred and shuttered windows and saw the high pulpit that had been set up for the Cardinal. Hours later the prelate mounted the pulpit and prepared to speak. Suddenly the Baal Shem commanded me, Moses, you go to the Cardinal and tell him to come here. Tell him the Baal Shem is here.

So I brazenly approached the Cardinal and said, Come, the Baal Shem is calling you.

I know he's there, the Cardinal said. You tell him I'll come after my sermon.

When I reported this to the Baal Shem, he said, Go back and tell him to come now.

I did, and lo and behold, the Cardinal excused himself from the thousands in the Square, and followed me into this heavily barred and shuttered house. There he and the Baal Shem were cloistered for a matter of two or three hours. Finally the two of them came out.

Look, the host broke in, I'll tell you the rest of the story. I know who you are. I recognized you when you came. Did you recognize me?

And Moses said, I do now. You were the Cardinal.

Yes. I was a former Jew who had risen high in the Catholic Church. When the Baal Shem called for me I know why. I gave up my persecution of the Jews, disappeared, and built a new life for myself. Now that you've come, I take this as a sign that I have been forgiven. The Baal Shem told me that when a man comes as his messenger some day, I will know that I have been forgiven and I can tell that messenger that his job has been completed, too, and that he can now go to the promised land and be free from his wanderings.

A third community with a meaning for us today is that of the Early Church, immediately following the death and resurrection of Christ.

This community was fired with the vision of a world that had been deteriorating, that was corrupt, rotten, on the verge of ultimate judgment. From this world each of the Church's members was rescued into a glorious joy of deliverance, of freedom, and of servitude to One who was so great and loving and worthy that it was an honor to be His slave. At the very moment one became a slave, one became a king. It was a community in which there was a concept of an overarching wholeness, a notion of a body in which no part was higher or lower or better or worse than another, but in which all parts were integral and meaningful to one another and to the whole.

And there was a feeling of belonging in a very focused sense to the revival of something very old, the culmination of something very ancient, namely, God's dealings with His people.

But now was added something altogether new, even though very ancient, something so inspiring that it was inflammatory; it shook those who were involved in it, and it could not but shake those who were outside it. They were shaken either to acceptance or to persecution. The nature of the legal, political, and religious situation of the time was such that the temper was not one to compromise. Whether it existed above or below the ground it drew its strength from a common center, Christ, a person whom they saw even when he was physically absent, a person whose life they felt dwelt in them, and a portion of whose body they felt they were. In such a situation there could not but be an oscillation between notions of perfection in everyday life that were believed to prepare one for an instantaneous translation into eternity, and counsels of a more practical, everyday, humdrum type that seemed to the Christians to be counsels of compromise and corruption. This oscillation led, of course, to the problem of who was in the "in-group" and who was in the "out-group" regarding redemption, and what the possibilities were for the person who'd fallen from the intimacy of the inner Christ.

The struggles between Christian and Jew, between those who had known the Lord in his earthly life and those who had not, between those for whom the vision was a transmutation of something pagan, and for those for whom the vision was a gradual change or evolution, were as real as the struggle between the redeemed and unredeemed. The amazing thing was that this community was able to survive, to *strengthen itself inwardly by a series of ideas* that were corporate and came to be the key words of the community's creed. There was baptism and the Eucharist; there was a special attitude toward the family as related somehow integrally to God's family. There arose a two-way process of defining a member. The word in the Scriptures is "confess."

But confession is not a private act. It is public. Confessing with the mouth the Lord Jesus is an act whereby one, in a sense, took Christ upon himself and invested himself in the body that was Christ's. It is an act of confirmation in a sense whereby the individual is confirmed by the community who said to him, "Yes, indeed, you are Christ's and we accept you," and he at the same moment, said, "I take Christ, I choose Christ, I invest my life or my death in Chirst."

The two-wayness of this act of confirmation is the key to true community, as against imposed community which is the pulling together of persons according to a principle that does not resonate with their own commitments. Confirmation goes on between both the community and the person confirmed. In the community of the Hasidim the Hasid confirms the Hasidim, the Hasidim confirms the Hasid—there's a two-wayness. Again in the little Senoi family, the father hears the dream and accepts it, and the child tells it without fear. In every community, the possibility of confirmation makes possible and opens the way to the possibility of community.

Community, then, depends upon confirmation by which one accepts an identity, and at the moment of accepting the identity, identifies the group which one accepts. You are now a Boy Scout, you are now a Christian, you are now a son—the community gives a name and in turn says, "You are valued and recognized."

To be confirmed then, is to be accepted as valued by a community that accepts and values, and a community that you accept and value. It's a two-way process and it's a process without which you are left alone, unrelated, and a nonentity even to yourself.

6 ❋

The Self in Hell

A patient of mine once dreamed that he was approaching a drawbridge in his automobile when the two arms parted and the bridge opened. After a ship had passed, the arms began to descend and my patient drove his car onto the one nearest him. Much to his surprise, his section did not come down to meet its partner, but rather swung forty-five degrees out to sea. My patient drove off the bridge into the bay.

While this dream had several meanings for him, one of them is particularly important for everyone. The failure of the separated parts to reunite represented an unwillingness to bring together two warring factions in himself. He refused to function as a bridge.

Each of us is a bridge. We link past and present, inner and outer, the corporate and the individual, time and eternity, infinite and finite, organic and inorganic, and good and evil in and around ourselves. When we fail as a bridge we are split, and when we are split we are in hell.

Hell is the separation of that which belongs together. It is a state of torment, of unnaturally forcing, twisting, or distorting parts that are meant to fit. It turns a drawbridge into a chasm.

When the bridge is in place, communication occurs between the separate dimensions of the self: individuality, relatedness, equilibrium, and motion. When the bridge is up or twisted out of fit, communication is severed or distorted. The messages the individual sends and receives sometimes seem to be terribly wrong.

Who among us has not endured the awful conviction that at some moment he was not himself, that he was the victim of a tendency over which he had no control, crying out in anguish even as did St. Paul, "The things that I would I do not, and the things that I would not, these I do?" When man is in such a state, he yearns for some explanation of this mystery. Man has always been tempted to project the rejected elements of himself onto others, to blame them for his own misdeeds, or to see the misdeeds as existing only in these others. In our society today, we are constantly witnessing attempts to attribute to another the unacceptable in oneself. For Hitler and the Nazis, Jews were the Satan-equivalent; for Communism, all non-Communists and revisionists. Conflicts, temptation, and inexplicable behavior are frequently ascribed to the Devil. An inexplicably persistent thought today is still called an obsession, a term that derived directly from ancient notions of demon possession.

But the truth is that hells exist not only outside the self, but also within. The self is in hell essentially because there is hell in the self. The isolated parts of the split-up self, seeking to go their own way, war on one another, and from time to time take over one another's function, leading to surprising impulsive outbursts. When this occurs, man frequently becomes a slave to some unbridged part.

This form of slavery we call neurosis.

Neurosis is a situation in which substitute expression of the deep, inner, alienated side of the self comes into expression in disguise. Then the dark side of the self may be experienced in symptoms, fears, obsessions, alteration of bodily functions, and weird experiences of unreality. These bizarre and otherwise unaccountable manifestations do reveal an aspect of the deep self, but they do it through a distorting lens. These disguised exiles, entering without a passport, are never acknowledged or recognized for what they really are, nor are they successfully repatriated and integrated.

Neurosis, like hell, is as old as man. Who does not remember the Old Testament story of Samson and Delilah? Samson was a judge of Israel, but his fame stemmed from the greatness of his strength. His feats of power in peace and war were fabulous. The secret of his strength was said to be in his hair. That is, the Spirit

of the Lord strengthened him as long as he observed the rule of
the Nazarites, which included allowing his hair to grow.

But Samson, who liked to play cruel jokes on others, had collected many enemies. His strength and cunning and sense of
humor had given them a strong desire for vengeance. Samson
knew this. More than once he had been deceived by a woman—
first his wife, who out of fear for herself and her father gave away
the answer to his riddle, and then left him for a friend; second,
by a harlot who was supposed to detain him while his enemies
waylaid him; third, and most familiar to us, by Delilah. Three
times, the account relates, Samson tested her with the alleged
secret of his strength; each time she attempted to unman him.
Nonetheless, her pleadings led him finally to give away his
secret. The outcome is well known. Delilah helped shave Samson's
head while he slept, then turned him over to his enemies who
blinded and imprisoned him. All that was left for Samson was the
final revenge of pulling down the pillars of the Temple on himself and on the whole host, killing more in his death than he had
in his life.

In some respects, all of us are Samsons. Time and again we
are deceived; time and again we participate in our own undoing.
Each time, on the slimmest of excuses, we go back for more—
and play into the hands of our enemies. Samson not only allowed
himself to be victimized, he created and provoked his enemies
by acts of gratuitous hostility.

Let us now recognize what Samson could not—that most of
our enemies are within us. When our desires are not integrated,
their satisfaction cannot be achieved. Samson hungered for love.
What is more natural than that? But with all his manliness he
could not accept the idea that part of him wished to be loved as
if he were a helpless child. By arranging to be shorn of his manly
strength, he actually brought his unconscious wish to fulfillment
—but with what tragic consequences!

Like Samson, we are all vulnerable to our inner hungers. And
like him, too, we conceal these hungers even from ourselves. We
seek substitute solutions, which we use as makeshift bridges.

These bridges exist in all of us. Few of us, admittedly, are aware that they do; were it not for the few for whom their existence makes life a nightmare, we might never know what they are like.

Here I am going to describe a few of these bridges created by man. While I will be illustrating with sick people—patients of mine or those of my colleagues—the principles illustrated apply even to those persons who are nominally healthy. Advanced symptoms exist in many of us to a less well-developed degree.

One of the most common of the substitutes for valid, unifying solutions is alcohol.

John Jones is successful at work, or so he believes. He brings home his check each month, receives periodic advancements, and is respected as a good worker and a "regular fellow." But it has been years since he dared to express an original idea, to object to an obvious absurdity in company practice, or to reconsider his vocation. Long ago he buried both his ideals and his dreams in compromise with what he felt to be the inevitable. Jones feels more "at home" while working than when he is with his family. His business demands are predictable, his responses are well learned and safe, and there are no growing and changing children to remind him of what he was and what he could have been. Jones's superiors are convinced that he is a well-adjusted junior executive. He is admired by his subordinates. There is just one problem he hasn't licked, and that is how to bridge the chasm from office to home at night. He is unaware that he uses alcohol as his makeshift bridge.

Jones commutes home each evening in a semistupor, just in time to give his children a bleary goodnight kiss, and to tolerate his wife during an hour or two of televiewing. Then he falls asleep.

It is not enough to say that Jones uses alcohol as a substitute for his mother's milk, of which he did not receive enough as an infant. It is not enough to say that the companionship he finds at bars is a substitute for friendships for which he never acknowledged the need as a child. Nor is it enough to say that he is so frightened by an overtrained, overstrict conscience that he uses alcohol to numb it. All this is true, but there is more.

At each decisive moment in the last twenty years, Jones has been selling short his freedom to choose between the difficult and the easy. At each new moment, because of past surrenders, he has less power of choice than before. In each new year, someone, usually his wife, has unspokenly filled the breech left by his diminishing courage. Jones's unconscious guilt over his failure to use his full self becomes worse and worse—and alcohol, five to ten shots daily—becomes the only means of concealment.

Alcohol and other drugs may temporarily give us the means to exhibit an aspect of ourselves that we otherwise hide. But is such a disclosure valid when it occurs under a partial anesthesia? While interesting and indeed valuable depths of the self may be revealed, what is important is *how* they are apprehended and worked into the conscious self that decides and wills and acts. If these depths are not so apprehended, the split in the self is only momentarily overcome. Rather than a victory, it is a truce occuring in a stupor.

Another common neurotic bridge is the replacement of real by imaginary fears.

Bill Benson fears bridges. Even though he works in a city with many of them he ingeniously manages to avoid them without revealing his irrational concern to his employer or customers. He is regarded by everyone as a normal, well-adjusted, successful man. Only his wife knows of his symptoms and she is pledged to secrecy. She *doesn't* know, however, what these fears really mean, although they involve her in ways she can dimly guess.

Bill Benson's father deserted his mother when he was three. In a sense, the foundations were removed from the bridge between his parents that he believed himself to be. Like most young children whose parents divorce, Bill blamed himself for the collapse of the bridge.

In his mind Bill remained a bridge, one that was now without parental foundation. Even so, he had now to extend it further; he had to be father as well as son to his family. Outwardly he made the grade. He was a loyal son to his mother, a loyal father to his younger brother. But inwardly his own identity as man and male was precarious, because he felt himself to be a coward. He did not know that his fear of bridges was a symbolic concern carried over from his own apparent collapse as a bridge between his parents.

Bill's shame affected both his sexual and religious life.

He became so concerned about each that the other suffered. Today he is unable to attend confession because he feels too embarrassed to admit his childish substitutes for marital sex relations. Yet he compulsively pursues that which makes him guilty. God for him is both the sadistic tyrant who threatens him with doom and at the same time an easily deceived policeman who winks at what is obvious. His wife blames herself for their sexual problems, and their children feel guilty for "making Daddy and Mother nervous." Bill could be different, but for years he has run away from the recognition of his false bridges and thus from his eventual liberation.

Examples of these ersatz bridges include other instances that modern psychiatry also calls neurosis. Escape into health—or the denial of pains and troubles to avoid facing them—is as neurotic a bridge as alcoholism. So is the deification of normality or conformity.

Roger Randall goes to dancing classes Tuesdays and Thursdays to acquire balance and poise. He attends success and personality school on Wednesdays to learn to adjust and succeed at work. He is worried that his wife, Mabel, is not well integrated because she has ideas and ways that are different from those of his co-workers' wives. Mabel resents the feeling that she has to conform but sees that Roger is devoutly committed to finding his place in society and filling it, and she supposes that sooner or later she'll have to give in.

The pursuit of adjustment, the superficial conformity to definitions of normality, the evasion of the depths by focus on the obvious, all lead to a life that merely touches the surface of full experience. People live roles, not lives. The deviant and the distinctive are attacked, and we become so busy being normal that we lose the richness and depth that our inner struggle for self-knowledge could yield. That illness may be a signal of truth, that superficial health may be an illusion masking sickness in our depths, is forgotten. As Socrates declared, the unexamined life is not worth living.

Pseudo-health is no better when it is gained through religion. Many hearken today to voices that promise health and happiness, peace and pleasure, success and adjustment as the reward for right thinking and doing. Such escapes bypass self-confrontation; they leave little self to sense a neighbor's anguish or depth, or to see God in His fullness of wrath and suffering forgiveness. Nor is religious practice that offers escape from the self through frenzied activity, pedantic preoccupation with details, or passive withdrawal from the world any better.

Other escapes may be corporate rather than individual. It may be easier, for example, to face uncertainty, shame, doubt, or guilt if others share them. There is always a danger in corporate confession, corporate reassurance, and corporate affirmation. Another's guilt makes ours less poignant, another's shame makes ours less painful, another's doubts make our less reprehensible. But only as we come to know our *own* doubt, shame, and guilt, only as we see that in some sense ours is different and personal, is it meaningful to talk about its relation to that of others. Otherwise we and they are talking about surface experiences.

But of all the devious methods we use to escape the obligation of bridging our parts, none, perhaps, is quite so ironic as when we refuse to recognize the greatness in ourselves. We pervert every good gift and call it evil. God gives us sex and we call it lust. He gives us aggression and we call it hate. He gives us curiosity and we call it arrogance. Seeing the good as evil makes us use it as evil—and ultimately deprives us of its use.

Jane Smith is a would-be artist. Her work seems unoriginal. Her creativity exists, but it appears in her dreams and fantasies, largely in a frightening form. She cannot give creative birth for she fears that what is inside her is evil—and the way she relates to it, it *is* evil. She constantly bemoans her fate but never takes steps to change. She behaves as if she prefers things as they are to the way they might be.

A glance at Jane's history reveals many clues to her fear of recognizing and using her talents. At five, she had begun to show talent for dancing; her mother, a professional dancer, encouraged her. As she improved, her teacher began to make extravagant prophecies about her future. To the normal jealousy every five-year-old feels toward her mother was thus added the rivalry of a prematurely promised dancing career. As is normal for five-year-olds, Jane assumed that her mother felt counter-rivalry and that her success would destroy her mother. In the midst of such fantasies, Jane's mother was killed in an automobile accident. Jane's dancing ceased; her talent was paralyzed.

Years later, Jane discovered a talent for art. But her stepmother was an artist, too. Rather than risk a second death for which she would blame herself, Jane allowed her talent to languish. All this was unknown to Jane while it happened. She learned of her unconscious rejection of her talents only after she had gone to a therapist. Jane's dilemma illustrates one of the most painful heritages of childhood—the deep inner belief that whatever we have, we have wrested from someone else. To a certain extent, this is true. There is nothing we ever have that we have not received. The mother's breast, the father's encouragement, the teacher's knowledge, the friend's acceptance—all are given. Somewhere along the line, most of us forget that all true receiving is actually a form of sharing. The giver receives in the giving. The moment this is lost sight of, receiving becomes grasping, and grasping a form of exploitation of the giver. To excel, therefore, becomes tantamount to destruction of those who have given us the most. It implies that we have depleted them in order to increase ourselves. Imagine then what this unconscious fear does to the child who is on the verge of surpassing his beloved parent. The conflict is further intensified if the parent urges the child on to success—to do, in other words, the very thing that will make the child feel guilty. Not only does the child feel sorry about hurting the cherished parent; his guilt is also an expression of the expectation of punishment. Every young child believes that wishes are omnipotent; he also believes in retribution; what he does will be done to him; therefore, the penalty for his success at some later date will be his well-deserved failure and downfall. Much later, as an adult, he connects achievement with competition and competition with destruction of a rival. Fearing retaliation or censure, he avoids competition and thus cuts himself off from achievement.

No better evidence of this unconscious attitude exists than in the manner Americans react to compliments. Instead of admitting honestly their pride in achievement, they belittle and deny it as if it were something to be ashamed of.

Here is a paradox! Here an irony! So complex is man that he fears the very success his inner strivings demand. Surely such deviousness he cannot help but view as a curse.

What is the source of this "curse"? What is its connection with the roots of evil? What, indeed, is the source of evil? Does it come from God? The Devil? One's neighbor? Oneself? Is evil inevitable, inescapable? Or is it an accident, and preventable?

God only knows. We do not. All we do know is that evil is everywhere around us. It is fruitless to ask where ultimately it comes from as a prerequisite to its proximate elimination. People who do are really asking, "How do you get around it?"

The problem is to deal with evil. How do we do that?

First of all, we recognize that evil exists—but as a perversion of the good. This does not mean denying that this perversion is radically destructive; that we suffer inwardly and cause others to suffer. It *does* mean that we are willing to take what we have called evil and use it in the service of good.

Second, we must reopen our receptivity to pain. To be truly alive is to be able to feel pain, both one's own and one's neighbors. Living is *not* the numbness of easy salvation, through thinking good thoughts or busying oneself in good works and important causes. As long as we live there will be suffering. But how do we use it? Do we deny its presence? Do we blame it on others? Do we relish and enjoy it, indeed perversely bring it upon ourselves? Or have we the wisdom and patience to avoid unnecessary suffering and to accept and use the inevitable suffering that may be our lot? The latter course is that of the wise man and the saint, the humble person who neither seeks out nor flinches from, pain.

Suffering—even the most apparently meaningless—can be used. A stirring document of its creative use is offered by Viktor Frankl, whom we considered earlier in connection with his book

From Death Camp to Existentialism.[1] Frankl tells how some inmates of his concentration camp gave up and welcomed death; how others expressed their bitterness in sadistic cruelty to their fellow prisoners; how still others found ways of learning from their pain something of the meaning of their own life, and the challenges life still held for them even in their apparently God-forsaken condition.

A third means of dealing with evil is to recognize our part in it, to realize that the demons are inside us. Most people do this by increasing their feelings of guilt. But calling ourselves guilty sinners, pleading guilty to every sin, serves as a substitute for a real examination of our lives. By preoccupation with guilt feelings we actually avoid discovering the aspects of ourselves that can and must be changed if our behavior is to be just and loving. The picayune cataloguing of individual vices may replace the awakening of radical concern for our total out-of-jointness with God, nature, neighbor, and self.

The too-easy confession of sins leads one to an impasse. Only that person who believes he is basically good can take responsibility for the evil in himself. To say one is a complete mess is to say one could have done no better, and that basically God made us bad. This attitude is reminiscent of the apology of the mouse berated by a lion for being small: "I'm sorry, I've been sick!"

The fourth and final decision we must make in an effort to deal with evil is to relate ourselves to others in a *personal* way, as persons not things. Failure to do this means withdrawal from the world and abdication to the imaginary foe.

Except for his mother no one ever sees Carl Carlton. Since he quit his job five years ago he's stayed at home; he has closed the door to any future. Her meager pension and his tiny savings support them. She has become worried about what will happen to him after she is dead, but he refuses to think of this possibility, apparently preferring to go on in the daze of isolated withdrawal. Once he allowed the minister in the house. That was two years ago. Now there is doubt whether he will leave except by police escort.

[1] Trans. Ilse Lasch (Boston: Beacon Press, 1959).

One can hardly say that he chooses or prefers his present condition. He is beyond choosing, for there was a time when, after a certain decision had caused him pain by revealing aspects of himself that he did not wish to confront, that he chose, in effect, not to choose.

Restoring Carl Carlton to the condition of free choice is the difficult task of a psychiatric team. Before he can feel pain creatively again, he may have to feel anger destructively, lust recklessly, despair wrackingly. The path he must now retrace is one that each of us must traverse. However arduous and dangerous, it is inescapable. We must partake of our world.

But extreme immersion in the world can be just as bad as extreme withdrawal. Mary Levitt had been so close to her group that she rarely could be distinguished from it. She put group loyalty before family, job, religion, or her own needs. In fact, the group had become all these for her, and was indistinguishable from them. When the group was branded criminal and subversive she was horrified and unbelieving, later tried suicide; her world had collapsed and she saw herself as having shared in its destruction.

Such immersion comes through exaggeration of the need to be a part. This symbiotic need is one we all feel; it is the residual of the normal child's dependence and the normal adult's need for affiliation. When the craving to *belong* overbalances the need to *differentiate* from the mass, the individual never becomes a self in his own right. As a child, Mary appeared to be an ugly duckling; her mother told her repeatedly that no man could love her because she was a freak. When a group appeared that would accept her, she was overwhelmed. She was also undiscriminating. One who is so hungry for the merest human affection can hardly be expected to behave as a connoisseur. Now, a recovering patient in a mental hospital, she has acquired esteem as a separate self.

Extremes are rarely gratifying as lifelong patterns. Passivity violates man's need for directed action and frenetic activity his need for centered equilibrium. Passivity and compliance do not constitute real participation and affirmation. Challenge and confrontation do not constitute independence and choice.

Yet even *ordered doing* has its dangers. Marvin Barker does everything energetically and well. He is forever finding new places to invest his many talents. He knows the world as his workshop and his arena of action. But receptiveness and openness to others and the inwardness of his quiet inner self are unknown to him. In his dreams, however, Barker sees visions of the broad, peaceful lands of reflection. He feels the cool winds of unforced being, of unhurried contemplation. This side of him deserves to be heard, but he is forever running from it. Here, again, is a fear of confrontation. Instead of withdrawal, Barker substitutes preoccupation.

Unlike the Senoi who accept their dreams as part of life, most of us isolate ourselves from messages which come through this medium. We are thereby cut off from the correctives that could help us to balance our lopsided lives, the correctives of the unheard inner voice. Failing to become whole, we seek adjustment. But adjustment occurs around a faulty salvation; in his search for himself man becomes less than himself. None of his efforts leads him up and out of a hell of destruction, or even into a hell of purification.

Most of these pseudo-hells can be transcended or escaped by seeing them for what they are. But that is not easy because they all mask the deeper reality, the greater crime or schism, the *separation* of the self from its deep inner rootage, from God Himself. Just as the pseudo-heavens can keep us from the King of Heaven, so the pseudo-hell can prevent our escape from the real hell.

These maneuvers away from reality have simply led us into greater and greater compression of our potential being, a compression which is at last approaching the point of explosion. For we live in an age that is starving, depressed, suicidal. True, we have prosperity here and there, and Americans like to imagine that others are either as well off as they, or on the road to economic and hygienic salvation. True, leisure and enjoyment of life have in some parts of our world reached a high peak for large masses, and an American workingman can enjoy his own car and television, and send his sons to college. True, we are on the verge of new discoveries that may conquer disease and prolong life, that may clarify the relevance of religion, make neurotic life less inevitable. But our health is a hazard if it distracts us from the doom with which we toy.

Never before have a few men owned the means of destroying the whole world. Never before have we seemed as blind to the real danger we possess and constitute for one another. Never before have we been as far from seeing any real and lasting solution to the problem of power, for we are suddenly possessed of power far beyond our judgment and wisdom and compassion. We were shocked when our own nation used it at Nagasaki and Hiroshima, but the shock did not last; rather, it seems to have benumbed us to the power that is increasing even *more* rapidly. Most of us are afraid to face this fact, sensing that the very knowledge itself would be destructive and unendurable. As Charles Williams has so well said, "It is habitual for us 'to prefer' to be miserable rather than to give, and to believe we could give our miseries up."

So, in a sense, hell has come to fruition. May we be wise enough to see what we must—that this hell is of our own making, that it springs from the hell within ourselves. We must learn to live with it or perish.

7 ✿

The Self in Communion

In one sense this book would end more realistically if we left the self in hell, where most of us surely are. Yet realism blind to the possibility of redemption is as unworthy as medicine blind to the possibilities of healing. As a psychiatrist I have been a participant in the process of healing, sometimes with gratification and sometimes with disappointment. Occasionally I have forgotten that it was not I who healed alone, but something within the patient and between us as well.

Only the physician who believes in a potential power for healing that exists within his patient can treat his patient. Whether he calls this power the *vis medicatrix naturae* (healing power of nature) or the *vis medicatrix dei* (healing power of God), the worthy physician has faith that the patient is fighting alongside him for health and against sickness. In a sense the physician can be only the assistant to this power, saying with Ambroise Paré, the "Father of French Surgery," "I dressed his wounds and God healed him," or with Sigmund Freud, the father of psychoanalysis, that we are the midwives participating in the birth of the healthy self.

But while it would be most unphysicianly for me to make none but gloomy conclusions, it would be just as unphysicianly for me to fail to give gloom its due. I am convinced that it is only in the perpetual recognition of the possibility of illness that health can be achieved even fleetingly, that illness can be prevented even partially.

I have already suggested that we die of loneliness and lovelessness when we make ourselves the center of our lives and do not live in participative community. I have suggested that we can only validate ourselves by giving them to others. It is the community that helps us confirm who and what we are; without it we have little identity.

But community as we ordinarily think of it is not enough. There is a condition of participation that goes beyond the community. Not only does it validate; it heals. This condition is called communion, *and it is the answer to hell.*

Communion means the relating of the parts, all the parts— good and evil, corporate and individual, divine and human. It is the curing of the split condition that we have come to know as hell. Historically, communion occurs in at least three senses: the communion of the saints, the communion of the Lord's Supper, and the communion that transcends symbols. Each points to the other.

The communion of the saints is a Christian term that has implications for those come together as a part of the Redemptive Community that the Church seeks to be and never quite becomes, and, in a union across time and space, of those who have either died or are yet to be born. This communion is a fellowship that cuts across race and creed and external affiliation in a reality we remember (or too often forget) on All Saints' Day and at funerals, and otherwise largely ignore.

The uniting principle of both aspects of this communion of saints is the belief that Christ showed man what he is, namely, one who can become himself only through bearing the burdens of others and allowing them to bear his burdens. Charles Williams, who exemplified this theme in life, always insisted not only that we must bear one another's burden but that no man can bear his own burden alone. This is one meaning of the Cross.

Communion in the Lord's Supper goes back to the Jewish Passover feast as the commemoration by the Hebrews of their liberation from slavery at the hands of the Egyptians. Many believed that it was the Passover meal with his disciples that was Jesus' last supper, and this very feast has been accepted by the Church as its commemoration of liberation.

The Lord's Supper has many meanings. Psychologically, there is communion among the participants, one with the other. Theologically, there is communion between each participant and the Founder of the Feast. A symbol of the transaction is the food, as basic and organic a symbol of ultimate nurture and of receptive thanksgiving as possible. And yet to this simple meaning is added the more personal one of the incorporation of the Host of the feast—or making Christ part of the self and the self part of Christ. The words of the commemoration, "This is my body," symbolically represent the continuity of his people with Christ, one which both nourishes and judges, because to be in continuity with Christ is to be condemned to the humilating glory of making real the bridge between nature and man, between things and persons.

Being a bridge constitutes man's glory and his torment. The glory is that he can commune. The torment is that when he does not commune, he and his world are divided, and that when he does, he and his world are judged—because it is just at the moment when man most keenly feels that he is and must be a bridge and a burden-bearer that he most keenly recognizes his failure. It is at the moment of recognition of his greatest possibility that man accepts the most radical judgment of himself. Little wonder that he then embraces any number of methods of avoiding the recognition that he is a bridge.

Religion is by and large the most popular defense against the unbearable judgments and joys that follow from such recognition. And what a strange religion it becomes through man's distortions. Man will become preoccupied with doing rather than being, with avoiding sins rather than with accepting his sinfulness, with pursuing sanctity without his neighbor or with coercing his neighbor into an unwilling common pursuit. He will even destroy the source of the communion by fighting over its theological meaning or its external form, destroying its fellowship by making it exclusive rather than inclusive. He may concentrate on right belief, which deteriorates into doctrinal assent, or on salvation by agreement. He may even pursue moral perfectionism as a graceless legalism, forgetting the "drunken miracle" (as Charles Williams terms the wine-producing for the festivity of the Cana feast) which was perhaps best rediscovered in semimodern times in the slightly intoxicated ecstasies of the Hasadic faithful. Since then austerity and pomp have too often replaced joy and spontaneity, and conformity and exclusivism have replaced the fellowship that could even include Judas.

Where distortions persist, the basic need of man remains unfulfilled. While both hell and heaven are within, the self cannot find them alone. There can be no salvation outside the Church (in its deepest meaning), not because the Church alone has the Word, but because a redemptive community is part of all redemption. Bearing another's burdens, casting one's burdens upon the Lord, taking up the Cross, dying to live and living to die, all these do not go on in isolation—they grow out of relationship to God and self through the fellowship of the redemptive community.

But the community is not always redemptive; and even when it may seem to be redemptive, it may tend to become a god in itself, leading to new idolatries. Every good tends to deteriorate into an evil when it is absolutized; or into an idol when it is deified. The highest that God has given us tends to become demonic when it is confused with God Himself.

St. Augustine reportedly once said, "This also is thou; neither is this thou." This saying is a double corrective. Whenever men fail to see the good in anything in creation, even that which appears to be evil, the first half—"This also is Thou"—stands in judgment. Whenever men make an idol of anything, even the highest and best, the second half—"Neither is this Thou"—calls it into question and dethrones it.

"This also is Thou," must always be balanced with "Neither is this thou," whether we call this the Protestant Principle[1] or Oriental wisdom. Or, putting it in the words of Nicolas Berdyaev, the Russian Orthodox theologian, "There is a church in the existential sense, which is community and fellowship, and there are churches which are objectifizations and social institutions. When the church, as objectifization and a social institution is regarded as holy and impeccable, then the creation of an idol and the slavery of man begins. . . . Man possesses the capacity for turning love for God and for the highest ideas, into the most terrible slavery."[2]

[1] Cf. Paul Tillich's *The Protestant Era* (Chicago: University of Chicago Press, 1948), pp. 161 ff.
[2] Nicolas Berdyaev, *Slavery and Freedom* (New York: Charles Scribner's Sons, 1944), p. 294 ff.

The third meaning of communion constitutes a category that many would call nontheological and nonreligious, if not antitheological and antireligious. It is the communion that unites in unspoken mutual recognition those who can speak and listen to one another at the intersection of the secular and spiritual worlds. These men are bridges of self to others' selves, whether or not they know it, because in their being they fulfill an openness to all possibilities; because communication happens in and through their openness, and because they have not interrupted their participation in *exchange* because of preoccupation with its *coinage*.

Such men are religious without knowing it. They can be in communion without distraction of the external signs of religion or philosophy, creed or liturgy. They may not even be aware of their functioning as bridges of communion. Those who have made absolutes of the externals may judge these silent communicants, but they cannot dislodge them from their contact with one another and reality. On the other hand, the silent communicant is in no position to judge the man for whom the externals are important because, interfused with spirit and power and love, they serve as means of communication and grace.

Karl Heim, the German philosopher-theologian, has described all individuals as bridges between two world spaces.

We stand in two spaces at once, spaces with contracting structures.

The one space is the space into which we have been born, together with all other beings. In this space we live and think and explore in accordance with the generally accepted methods of natural science together with all the others. We can communicate with all other human beings in a way which ensures mutual comprehension and general agreement. The second space is that which is disclosed to us only by a "second birth," as it were by a "second sight." With regard to this second space we can communicate only with those who have undergone the same experience as ourselves.[3]

Yet once this openness in both directions has been affirmed, the person so experiencing and affirming becomes a means of Grace. Such persons are *in* Grace; their lives communicate a

[3] Karl Heim, *Christian Faith and Natural Science* (New York: Harper & Brothers, 1953), p. 248.

gracious openness that does not insist on payment in advance. They are open to receive as well as to give, to be healed as well as to heal, to be forgiven as well as to forgive.

Forgiveness means that both must be forgiven because to forgive is an affront which the forgiven must endure and in turn forgive. Only in Grace, a dimension that can tolerate the absurd and the comical, the blessed and the whimsical, can this happen. Grace is a gift, but as Aldous Huxley has said, too often men pursue the gift when they have not accepted that which has already been given.[4] The given is our own self and the selves of others, the mystery and glory and torment of our own being, and the mystery and wonder and inscrutable awfulness of others. Says Huxley:

> That the infinite must include the finite and must therefore be totally present at every point of space, every instant of time, seems sufficiently evident. To avoid this obvious conclusion and to escape its practical consequences, the older and more rigorous Christian thinkers expended all their ingenuity, the severer Christian moralists all their persuasions and coercions.
>
> This is a fallen world, proclaimed the thinkers, and nature, human and subhuman, is radically corrupt. Therefore, said the moralists, nature must be fought on every front—suppressed within, ignored and depreciated without.
>
> But it is only through the *datum* of nature that we can hope to receive the *donum* of Grace. It is only by accepting the given, *as it is given*, that we may qualify for the Gift. It is only through the facts that we can come to the primordial Fact.[5]

Grace can be commanded no more than love. Each happens; there are conditions which may foster or hinder their happening, but we do not and cannot conjure up or manipulate their appearance. True healing cannot be magical; one cannot manipulate another magically even if this manipulation be dignified by the name of science or religion. What we *can* do is to open ourselves to participation in the life of communities and their communions, by whatever name; and to remember that openness is a condition that is required of one's own being as well as another's. Or as

[4] *The Devils of Loudun*, pp. 285 ff.
[5] *Idem.*

Gabriel Marcel, the French Catholic existentialist might have put it, "the need for Being is the need to participate, as contrasted with fitting into a routine."[6]

But this participation means risking the radical danger of losing the self, and what may be more frightening, of finding the self. The self we find may not be the kind of self we thought we wanted to be. It will surely not be the kind of self that was closed to the possibilities of evil, nor the kind of self that could imagine it was whole because it had exiled the internal rebels. Neither will the community of such selves be able to imagine that it is whole simply because it has banished its visionaries to mental hospitals or monasteries and its nonconformists to prisons.

In both individual and collective forms, this kind of open self will perpetually risk destruction; it will live at the edge of an abyss; the abyss will be frightening, but the self will have learned to live with the fear because it will have known the depth of the abyss, and will have discovered that part of the rejected self returns as a blessing rather than a curse.

How much any one of us can risk this kind of openness is problematic. To propose that it is an easy possibility is to give false hope. But to deny that it is a possibility is to deny all hope.

The varieties of pseudo-hell and pseudo-transcendence all lead to some violation of the basic qualities of the whole self—relatedness, individuality, equilibrium, and action. Escape into mob psychology, for example, violates individuality, escape into isolated meditation violates relatedness, escape into inactivity violates directedness, escape into frenetic activism violates centeredness. Yet each man will express each of his dimensions in a personal way. The ways may seem contradictory, but the man in pilgrimage prays for grace to recognize his brethren in pilgrimage and to respect the way each of them must travel to achieve full selfhood.

Grace does not mean live-and-let-live indifference. Interaction is part of relatedness; it may be or seem to be negative interaction.

To realize that our fellowship can sometimes be uncomfortable is, of course, to face our anger and hurt as our own. Recognizing that even passive resistance constitutes an attack and acknowledg-

[6] Paraphrase from David Roberts, *Existentialism and Religious Belief* (New York: Oxford University Press, 1957), p. 283.

ing that from time to time we do and must attack one another is part of accepting and being the whole self, not rejecting the dark, nether underside. It means sharing in the responsibility for the individual and the collective wrongs we all commit and suffer. The threat of imminent nuclear destruction of ourselves, our genes, and our descendants, the "crime against the future," is so close as to be terrifying and paralyzing. We have neither the assurance of technological defense and prevention nor the promise of moral transcendence that would be the more radical and lasting solution. It is humbling to understand that not only *we* are on the brink of annihilation but also all we have built, begun, bequeathed, and even dreamed. Yet we seem to move on, almost as though we were not next door to doom. Is this denial a mechanism of defense, a flight from fear, an innate inability to contemplate the hour of mankind's death? Or is it the reflection of a hope within, a hope that witnesses to the innate organic assurance that life is good, that life is of God, and that He will not allow His creation to perish again as it did at the time of the Flood?

Perhaps there is a man in our world so placed that his courage will transcend faintheartedness; his clarity of thought, muddled thinking. Perhaps in him may come to focus the hopes and prayers and would-be achievements of the wishing billions. Perhaps he is not one specific man, but rather Everyman, facing the ultimate test of his existence—his willingness to become a saving incarnational bridge.

Jewish mythology describes the exile of the Shekinah, or the glory of God from the creation. May this not be analogous to the exiles of the forbidden side of man's self and the creation of an artificial split in his nature? Not only man is split by this division and exile, but God, as well; the ultimate restoration of the exiles is also the restoration of God to His wholeness and to His glory. Perhaps as we come to accept the hitherto unacceptable in our world, we will come to accept even in our God the negative that until now we have invested in the Devil, whom we ourselves have empowered as our enemy and God's enemy, and whose exile we have enforced at the cost of depleting ourselves and our God. We have accepted the symbol of final defeat of a part of

God's universe as foreordained and irreversible. We have built hedges around the holy, and in so doing have destroyed not only the holy but also that which it must hallow. We have accepted the demonic verdict of ultimate separation instead of accepting the ultimate reality of reunion.

To be sure, we have wanted reunion and sometimes have even pretended that it had already come to be. But reunion does not come about through denying difference and separation. Reunion occurs, not by projecting demons onto the enemy, but by recognizing our own part in the suicide of the race. The price of the angels is the demons, and we may find it as hard to accept the former as the latter. Receiving the unearned gift of Grace may be more difficult than remaining brave in the face of injustice. Grace from our enemies may be more unwelcome than their assaults.

The forgiver is an offense, a scandal, a Christ; one who must realize that to forgive is to offer the grandest insult, that it involves working through the hostility of the forgiven toward the forgiver. Yet this is the only route to reconciliation. This is the shedding of blood, the risking of the forgiver's life, without which there is no forgiveness. Forgiveness of our enemies is the only solution to global paranoia, the projection of doubt and suspicion and ill motives upon one another, a mechanism that is at once a sign of our own poor self-perception and our own too excellent perception of others. This is what Jesus meant in his saying about the mote and the beam. He pointed out the incongruity in attacking our neighbor's blindness, the sliver (mote) in his eye—all the while having a log (beam) in our own eye. The mote is there, but we see it precisely *because* of the beam.

But before we can forgive others we must accept forgiveness. And we must forgive ourselves. This means that we really see and bewail the beam, that we really take steps to remove it, that then and only then can we stop feeling guilty and start being helpful.

Albert Schweitzer has called us to relinquish our nuclear power and to submit to tyranny rather than to use it as a threat, even a defensive threat, the risk of which may be total and final destruction of the human race. His alternative is not an easy one. The tyranny we would face might prove to be more terrible for ourselves and our descendants than any tyranny that the world has known. Yet Christianity was certainly healthier and more Christian as a persecuted minority religion. Judaism has certainly displayed its spiritual strengths more dramatically under dispersion and persecution than in moments of conquest.

How can we ever find the healing for ourselves and our enemies that comes only through self-surrender as long as we are deluded into believing that we are already or are about to be conquerors? This self delusion undermines us both as warriors and as healers, as conquerors and as conquered, and is rapidly becoming the prelude to annihilation.

Some form of redemption is necessary as the only alternative to suicide. What steps are we taking, then, to prepare for the inevitable partial surrender to our enemies—so that they may partially surrender to us? How can we accept the evil in ourselves as a prelude to accepting it in others?

It is our refusal to face our guilt, our contentment with the confession of lesser crimes, that has blocked our way to reconciliation. We have created our Armageddon, we have poured out our own vials of wrath. We have placed ourselves in a position where only God can save us; at the same time we have carefully disposed of the God who could. We are like children testing the limits of their parents' patience and endurance, seeing whether the parent will intervene, perhaps as a sign that the parent is really there, that the child really matters, and that the parent is powerful enough to extricate the child from his own dilemmas.

This is risky flirtation with destiny, with death, and with the Almighty.

Yet a Church that is afraid to speak peace to power, a State that cannot listen to psychiatry or religion, a psychiatry and a religion both of which can diagnose and neither of which is ready to risk entering the pesthouse, cannot rescue a perishing world. Our pride in not having failed because of not having tried is one deterrent to the needed action. Our fear of failure is another. Our belief, born of this fear, that the destiny of man is safer in the hands of statecraft, even paranoid statecraft, of military power, even frightened military power, is a third.

But if we know anything about human beings and their interactions—and this has been the business of religion and medicine for millenniums and of psychiatry for centuries—we know that fear and hate destroy and that love and forgiveness heal. If we believe in them at all we must entrust ourselves to them altogether —for they are unconditional in their demands. Even as hate and guilt and fear destroy the mind and the brain's effectiveness, so love and faith and hope enhance them. Even as isolation and tension destroy relationship, so interaction and earnest engagement build it up. These are simple truths built into the stuff of our lives and veiled to us only by the blindness to which we willfully cling. God did build love into the warp and woof of the universe—it did not creep in unawares. But the discovery of the given, the *datum,* the real truth that we all have received more love than we knew—this is the burden of forgiveness which means accepting, which means taking.

Reunion of enemies can only come about through mutual forgiveness, and its cost is staggering. We have all been terribly wounded by others' attempts to restore relationship. But the meaning of pilgrimage is a life that feels the offenses, in their fullest degree, yet continues with others in communion.

This questing communion may receive its symbols from history and the Scriptures, or may live without symbols, fearing to make of them idols. The miracle is that to some extent each type of communicant will see that the way of the other is the necessary corrective to its own, just as every moment in which we imagine we see God in another person, event, or part of ourselves, we must be corrected by the reminder, "Neither is this Thou"; when we imagine that something unfamiliar, unknown, or unwelcome is not God or of God, we must be corrected by the reminder, "This also is Thou." Whether our way is an affirmation of images, with symbols right and left that cast a glorious spectrum over a drab and desolate world, or whether we reject every idol, attractive as it may be, demanding that our God be ineffably pure and transcendent, we will be both right and wrong. But we will be in communion, and to be in communion is to be in pilgrimage.

INDEX

Abraham, 19
Acceptance, meaning of, 61; *see also* Empathy; Forgiveness; Grace; Hostility; Love; Peace; Resonate; Sex; Spontaneity; Stimulus
Adolescence, 50-53; as a "witchcraft period," 51; *see also* Psychological Development; Self
Alcoholism, 84-85; *see also* Psychiatry; Neurosis
America, 3; "Ideal" of, 8; social creed of, 5
Anglicus, Bartholomeus, 29
Anxiety, 8; *see also* Evil; Fear; Good and Evil; Hell; Pain; Sin
Apocryphal writings; see Scripture
Augustine, 4, 97
Autism, 52-53, 60 f.; meaning of, 36; *see also* Psychological Development; Self

Baal Shem Tov, 76-78
Baptism, 67-68, 79
Belloc, Hilaire, 71
Benedek, Theresa, 47
Berdyaev, Nicolas, 97
Bettelheim, Bruno, 63
Between Man and Man, 64 n.
Bible: see Scripture
Birth, double aspect of, 37; *see also* Psychological Development; Self
Body, ix; Greek view of, 16; and spirit, 17 f.; *see also* Psychosomatic; Self

Booth, Gotthard, 32
Bromberg, Walter, 28 n.
Buber, Martin, 64, 71

Canon Episcopi, 29
Casserley, J. V. Langmead, 13, 21 n.
Childhood, 42 ff.; *see also* Psychological Development; Self
Christ, 20 f., 30, 95-96; as second Adam, 23; and community, fellowship with, 69; and idea of personality, 23; perfection of, 23-24; mind of, 74; sexuality of, 23; work of, 96; as forgiver, 102; *see also* Jesus
Christian Faith and Natural Science, 98 n.
Christian in Philosophy, The, 13 n., 21 n.
Christianity, 8, 103; Christian, 95, 99; Christians, 20, 74; *see also* Communion of saints; Church; Koinonia; Protestant; Roman Catholic
Christology, 22 f.; *see also* Christ; Jesus
Chronicle, Salimbene's, 54
Church, 28, 31, 78-80, 95-97, 103-104; early church, 23, 24, 68-70; *see also* Christianity; Communion of saints; Koinonia; Protestant; Roman Catholic
Church and Mental Health, The, 32 n.

Good and Evil (*cont.*)
Anxiety; Evil; Fear; Hell; Pain; Sin
Grace, x, 70, 98 f., 100 f., 102; and non-verbal communication, 62; as surprise, 70; *see also* Acceptance; Empathy; Forgiveness; Hostility; Peace; Resonate; Sex; Spontaneity; Stimulus; Love
Gratian, 29
Greeks, 12; philosophy of, 8, 11, 16, 19, 20 n.; religion of, 15-16
Guilt, 30-31, 69, 85 f., 103, 104; *see also* Psychiatry

Hasidism, 75-78, 80, 96
Healing, 6-7, 68-69, 99, 103, 104; as openness to surprise, 70
Hebb, Donald, 55
Hebraic-Christian tradition, ix, 8, 9; *see also* Hasidism; Hebrews; Israel; Messiah; Jews
Hebrews, 17 f., 20 n.; *see also* Hasidism; Hebraic-Christian tradition; Israel; Jews; Messiah
Heim, Karl, 98
Hell, 81-94, 95; definition of, 81-82; pseudo-hells, 92-93; answer to, 94-104; *see also* Anxiety; Evil; Fear; Good and Evil; Pain; Sin
Henry, George W., 20 n.
History of Medical Psychology, 20 n., 28 n.
Homeric Gods, 13 n.
Hostility, 9, 69, 71 f., 104
Humaneness, 12-13
Huxley, Aldous, 28 n., 99

I and Thou, 64
Iliad, 13 n.
Incubi, 28
Indian, East, 12, 17; religion of, 17, 53
Infancy, 36 f.; tempo of, 38-39; *see also* Psychological development; Self
Infanticide, 11
Inquisition, 28, 31
Israel: Its Life and Culture, 19 n.
Israel, prophets of, 22; *see also*

Hebraic-Christian tradition; Hebrews; Jews; Messiah

Jesus, 20 n., 21 f., 71, 74, 102; and God, 22 f.; parable of the talents, 7; parable of the vineyard, 43; *see also* Christ; Christology
Jews, 75-78, 95, 101, 103; obediance of, 8; saying of, 67; *see also* Hasidism; Hebraic-Christian tradition; Hebrews; Israel; Messiah

Koinonia, 69; *see also* Christianity; Communion of saints; Church; Protestant; Roman Catholic
Kraemer, 27

Levy, David, 46
Lilly, John, 55
Limitations, meaning of, 61
Lord's Supper; *see* Eucharist
Love, 7, 9, 30, 69, 71-72, 83, 97, 99, 104; *see also* Acceptance; Empathy; Forgiveness; Grace; Hostility; Peace; Resonate; Sex; Spontaneity; Stimulus

Magic, 25
Malleus Maleficarum, 27, 28, 31
Man above Humanity, 28 n.
Mass; *see* Eucharist
Matter, Mind and Spirit, 11 n.
Maturity, concepts of, 4; *see also* Psychological development; Self
Mead, George Herbert, 59
Messiah, 21, 75
Middle Ages, 25 f.
Mothering, 37 f.; *see also* Psychological development; Self
Muilenburg, James, 19 n.

Nature, powers of, 25
Neurosis, definition of, 82; *see also* Psychiatry
New Testament; see Scripture

Odyssey, 13 n.
Oedipus Complex, 48; *see also* Psychological development; Self
Oldham, J. H., 64